Disregard of the Corporate Fiction and Allied Corporation Problems

Disregard of the Corporate Fiction and Allied Corporation Problems

By

I. Maurice Wormser
PROFESSOR OF LAW, FORDHAM UNIVERSITY
EDITOR OF THE NEW YORK LAW JOURNAL

BeardBooks
Washington, D.C.

New York:

Baker, Voorhis and Company

Copyright, 1927 by L Maurice Wormser

Reprinted 2000 by Beard Books, Washington, D.C.

ISBN 1-58798-078-9

Printed in the United States of America

Foreword

THE corporate fiction, in regard to its true nature and proper application, is a vital subject. The multitude of discussions of it illustrates its fascination. The vast array of decisions dealing with it demonstrates its practical importance. So great a jurist as Mr. Justice Holmes has cautioned against allowing the fiction to become a "non-conductor" at the wrong time and place. The ebb and flow of the opinions on this phase of the law are most striking. As early as 1912 the author became interested. The consequence was his article, "Piercing the Veil of Corporate Entity." From time to time further papers were written. In 1927 the continued growth of his interest was evidenced by the delivery of an address, "Disregard of the Corporate Fiction—When and Why." He is hopeful that the suggestions contained in these pages may be of some slight help, and perchance serve at times as a guide to the perplexed.

Some of the subject matter has appeared in law reviews. The place of original publication is specified at the head of each paper. Grateful acknowledgment is made to the editors of the reviews for permitting reprinting, as well as to the Association of the Bar of the City of New York, under whose auspices the first of the following papers recently was delivered.

I. M. W.

New York, November 25, 1927.

Contents

Table of Cases

ix

TABLE OF CASES

TABLE OF CASES

xi

TABLE OF CASES

TABLE OF CASES

TABLE OF CASES

TABLE OF CASES

TABLE OF CASES

TABLE OF CASES

TABLE OF CASES

TABLE OF CASES

TABLE OF CASES

TABLE OF CASES

Disregard of the Corporate Fiction— When and Why [1]

IN an address delivered before this Association on October 25, 1923,[2] I had occasion to say that most of the criticism of legal science is unjust; that the manner in which the law develops demonstrates its ability to extricate itself from difficulties and to set forth with precision and with truthfulness the principles which govern our intricate network of present-day interests. It is true that lawyers too often lag behind the law and that the law too often lags behind our complex society. Yet, on the whole, the law has proven to be a steady and developing growth, sloughing off bad precedents whenever necessary and making new ones in response to alterations in mature public opinion. All in all, it is the best and wisest system of jurisprudence which the human race has ever developed.

[1] An address delivered by request before the Association of the Bar of the City of New York on the evening of November 10, 1927. Hitherto unprinted.

[2] Reprinted in 23 Columbia Law Review, 702-15 (Dec., 1923).

DISREGARD OF CORPORATE FICTION—

The development of corporation law furnishes a striking illustration of the ability of the law to move in spite of every effort, whether by subtle lawyer or by overreaching layman, to restrain it. In particular, the attitude of the courts toward the corporate fiction shows that they prefer the attainment of justice to any slavish adherence to a technicality or a syllogism.

In the introductory passage to Otto Gierke's "Genossenschaftstheorie," which is a valuable contribution both to jurisprudence and to sociology, it is said: "What man is he owes to association among men." [3]

President Butler of Columbia voiced the same thought when he declared in an address [4] that "the limited liability corporation is the greatest single discovery of modern times," and that "even steam and electricity are far less important than the limited liability corporation, and they would be reduced to comparative impotence without it. * * * It substitutes co-operation on a large scale for individual, cut-throat, parochial competition. It makes possible huge economy in production and in

[3] Berolzheimer, World's Legal Philosophies, pp. 368-9 *et seq.*

[4] Cyclopedia of Law of Corporations, Fletcher, Vol. I, p. 43 (from Ch. 1 by Wormser).

trading * * * it means the only possible engine for carrying on international trade on a scale commensurate with modern needs and opportunities." Certain it is that the number and importance of corporations are daily increasing. In size they range from the most insignificant to the gigantic American Telephone & Telegraph Co., with its 421,000 stockholders and its authorized capital of $1,500,000,000.[5]

Just what the corporation is, no two legal authorities are in accord. Definitions are dangerous. While I have no desire to enter into the philosophy of the subject, it should be observed that there are a number of very distinct theories, each hopelessly repugnant to the others. The German, or association theory, which has such an eminent English follower as Sir Frederick Pollock, views a corporation almost as a natural person and regards it as acquiring an "organic character which qualifies it to participate prominently in the life of the state and in the law."[6] I doubt, however, whether even the most advanced German philosopher would seriously argue that a corporation could marry or be given in marriage, or that it could vote at an election.

[5] Moody's Manual of Investments, 1927.
[6] Berolzheimer, World's Legal Philosophies, p. 370.

DISREGARD OF CORPORATE FICTION—

Yet, even in this country, corporations have been convicted for so purely personal crimes as grand larceny and the knowing and intentional deposit of obscene matter in the mails.[7] Under the association theory, the corporation acquires, therefore, an independent collective legal personality.

With this theory must be sharply contrasted the so-called fiction theory which regards the corporation as "*persona ficta.*"[8] The German philosopher regards this view as surviving only through inertia. Yet it finds embodiment in nearly all the law books, both in England and America. Perhaps its most classical embodiment is integrated in Chief Justice Marshall's definition in the celebrated case of *Dartmouth College* v. *Woodward,*[9] where he defined a corporation as "an artificial being, invisible, intangible, and existing only in contemplation of law." Doubtless Marshall gleaned the idea either

[7] *United States* v. *New York Herald Co.,* 159 Fed. 296; *United States* v. *MacAndrews & Forbes Co.,* 149 Fed. 823; see, also, cases collected in Canfield & Wormser's Cases on Private Corporations (2d ed.), pp. 22–3, footnote 8; also, Edgerton, "Corporate Criminal Responsibility," 36 Yale Law Journal, 827–44 (April, 1927).

[8] *Procter & Gamble Co.* v. *Newton,* 289 Fed. 1013, 24 Harvard Law Review, 253, 347.

[9] 4 Wheat. 518, 636; see, also, *Bank of the United States* v. *Deveaux,* 5 Cranch 61, 86, *per* Marshall, Ch. J.

from Lord Coke, who refers to a corporation as "invisible, immortal, and resting only in intendment and consideration of the law," [10] or from Mr. Justice Blackstone, who throughout his work refers to corporations as "artificial persons" or "artificial personalities." [11] Another embodiment of the fiction theory is found in the language of the late Judge Vann of the Court of Appeals of New York, who said: "A corporation, however, is a mere conception of the legislative mind. It exists only on paper through the command of the legislature that its mental conception shall be clothed with power." [12]

A learned law professor in this country has said that while the corporation is a fiction, in so far as the law treats it as a "person" it is "not a fiction in the sense of a supposition contrary to and having no relation to fact." [13] Or, expressed perhaps more simply, he may mean that it is a fiction which is not a fiction,—a thought my mind finds it difficult to follow.

A New York judge has recently suggested that a corporation is neither a reality, a personality, nor a

[10] Case of Sutton's Hospital, 10 Co. Rep. 1, 32.
[11] 1 Bl. Comm. 467-8.
[12] *People* v. *Knapp*, 206 N. Y. 373, 381.
[13] The Scope and Limits of the Corporate Entity Theory, 17 Columbia Law Review, 128, 129.

fiction, but "that a corporation is more nearly a method than a thing," and is merely "a name for a useful and usual collection of jural relations." [14]

Mr. Justice Oliver Wendell Holmes, undoubtedly the greatest jurist of our times, wrote to me on Dec. 19, 1923, that he regards the conception of corporate personality as a fiction, adding, however, "but as I said when young, on the Massachusetts bench, the very meaning of the fiction is that you are to act as if it was true."

After listening to all this fusillade, most of you will doubtless exclaim, with Warwick in Shakespeare's King Henry VI,

> "But in these nice, sharp quillets of the law,
> Good faith, I am no wiser than a daw."

Where the wise men differ, how can the layman be expected to see the light?

The late John Chipman Gray of Harvard, with the good sense that always characterized his utterances, said in his book on the Nature and Sources of the Law, that he would not undertake to solve the problem whether a corporation is "a real or only a fictitious entity," because "everybody is born either a Nominalist or a Realist." I am not

---

[14] *Farmers' Loan & Trust Co.* v. *Pierson*, 130 Misc. Rep. 110, 116–7, 222 N. Y. Supp. 532, *per* Bijur, J.

sure, however, that this is the best way of disposing of the problem, though assuredly it is the
easiest one.

It seems to me that a corporation may be correctly defined as a group of one or more persons
authorized by sovereign authority to act as a unit
and a personality in the eye of the law.[15] I cannot
bring myself to believe that a corporation which
"can level mountains, fill up valleys, lay down
iron tracks and run railway cars on them" [16]
is "a mere conception of the legislative mind,"
or that it is a mere "artificial being invisible, intangible and existing only in contemplation of law,"
or that it is only an "invisible, intangible essence
of air." But neither, on the other hand, can I
bring myself to believe that a corporation is a person in the sense that Gierke and Pollock view it,
with a personality akin to that of humans. It
has always seemed to me that a corporation, in one
sense, is a reality, as truly as is an army, a class
in a college or any other collective unit. Nobody
who has ever heard a college class dismissed would
doubt that it is a collective unit. It can be both

[15] Wormser, Law of Private Corporations, 4 (Blackstone
Institute, Chicago, Ill., 1914).

[16] *N. Y. Central & Hudson R. R. Co.* v. *U. S.*, 212 U. S. 481;
Bishop, New Criminal Law, § 417.

seen and heard. Suppose it incorporates in order to perpetuate its traditions,—does it become any the less a reality? Does it not still subsist as a collective unit? Whatever of "fiction" or of "paper existence" is involved in the conception of the corporation is found in the fact that the law endows the corporation with personality. A reality the corporation is. A personality the corporation is not. Gierke is quite correct in holding that the corporation has a will of its own and a volition identifiable from the individual volitions of the stockholders. Where he slips, to my mind, is in the fact that he attributes general personality to the corporation. This is traveling too far. It is pressing the bubble till it bursts.[17] The corporation is not really a personality. The law treats it as such, for purposes of convenience. The law, in other words, authorizes the corporation to act in many respects as though it were a natural person—which assuredly it is not—except in the contemplation and intendment of law. Only in this respect and to this extent is there anything of fiction involved in the corporate conception.

Since the element of personality is an extraor-

[17] *Cf. White, Executor*, v. *Bluett*, 23 L. J. Rep., Exchequer (N. S.), 36.

WHEN AND WHY

dinary privilege conferred upon the corporation by the law, and involves the employment of a fiction, it follows that "it must be used for legitimate business purposes and must not be perverted,"[18] and, just as night follows day, so the courts should and will disregard this fiction "when it is urged for an intent or purpose not within its reason and policy." [19]

Even the most careful jurist must constantly be on his guard in this respect. As great a lawyer as Mr. Justice Holmes wrote me: "Twice lately I have had to guard against the corporate fiction becoming a non-conductor in the wrong place," referring to *U. S. Grain Corp.* v. *Phillips*, [20] and to *U. S.* v. *Walter*.[21] All fictions of law are introduced for the purpose of convenience and to subserve the ends of justice. When they are urged to an intent and purpose not within the reason and

[18] 13 Calif. Law Rev. 235; see, also, valuable note, 36 Yale Law Journal, 254–60 (Dec., 1926), approving *Bressman, Inc.*, v. *Mosson*, 127 Misc. Rep. 282, 215 N. Y. Supp. 766; and *State Trust & Savings Bank* v. *Hermosa Land & Cattle Co.*, 240 Pac. (N. Mex.) 469.

[19] 13 Calif. Law Rev. 235; *Farmer's Loan & Trust Co.* v. *Pierson, supra.*

[20] 261 U. S. 106, decided Feb. 19, 1923, opinion *per* Mr. Justice Holmes.

[21] 263 U. S. 15, decided Oct. 22, 1923, opinion *per* Mr. Justice Holmes.

DISREGARD OF CORPORATE FICTION—

policy of the fiction, they must be disregarded by
the courts.[22] "It is a certain rule," said Lord
Mansfield when Chief Justice of England,[23] "that
a fiction of law shall never be contradicted so as
to defeat the end for which it was invented, but
for every other purpose it may be contradicted."
Fictions are invented and instituted for the ad-
vancement and promotion of justice, and will be
applied for no other purpose.[24] No sound reason
can be perceived why the principles applicable to
fictions in general should not apply to the fiction
that a corporation is a person in the eye of the law.
A person *in fact* it is *not;* a person *in law* it *is*, except in cases where the fiction is urged for perverted and fraudulent purposes.

A federal court has recently said, in language
peculiarly apt, "Every question of law arises out
of a fact situation, and if there be no state of facts
there can be no question of law." [25] The lawyer

[22] *State* v. *Standard Oil Co.*, 49 Oh. St. 137, 30 N. E. 279;
Wormser, "Voting Rights and the Doctrine of Corporate
Entity," 2 Fordham Law Rev. 21, 29; see, also, Broom's
Legal Maxims, 130.

[23] *Johnson* v. *Smith*, 2 Burr. 962; *Mostyn* v. *Fabriges*, Cow-
per, 177. See, also, *Morris* v. *Pugh*, 3 Burr. 1243.

[24] *Wood* v. *Ferguson*, 7 Oh. St. 291; *State* v. *Standard Oil
Co., supra; Rossman* v. *McFarland*, 9 Oh. St. 381.

[25] *United States* v. *Rodenbough*, 14 Fed. (2d) 989, 990.

has a creed. The judges are the transmitters and interpreters of that creed. The manner in which they accomplish this is through the decision of cases. One may begin the study of legal problems with a search for a general point of view.[26] One ends always with the consideration of cases. If one once understands the facts, the law flows almost inevitably from their mere statement. To state most legal problems fully and fairly is to answer them in advance. There is far more difficulty in ascertaining the facts than in applying the law. Therefore, I shall have to ask you to bear with me while I discuss cases as well as principles.

Now, easily the most distinctive attribute of the corporation is its existence in the eye of the law as a legal entity and artificial personality distinct and separate from the stockholders and officers who compose it, whereas a partnership, in legal contemplation, is simply the sum total of the partners.[27] This thought deserves elaboration, in order to understand the true application of the corporate fiction.

First, if a partner dies, the partnership terminates. It is automatically dissolved. The cor-

---

[26] Holmes, Collected Legal Papers, at p. 246.
[27] Clark, Corporations (3d ed.), 5-22.

poration, however, continues despite the death of a shareholder or his transfer of his stock. As Mr. Justice Blackstone aptly states in his Commentaries,[28] in speaking of a corporation, "All the individual members that have existed from the foundation to the present time, or that shall ever hereafter exist, are but one person in law, a person that never dies: in like manner as the river Thames is still the same river, though the parts which compose it are changing every instant."

Second, in a partnership, unless otherwise provided, each partner is an agent for the firm and his acts are binding upon the firm. A corporation, on the other hand, is managed by its duly elected board of directors and officers. The acts and contracts of the individual stockholder cannot bind the corporation.

Third, a partnership can be created by mere agreement of the parties. A corporation, however, cannot be constituted by the mere agreement of the incorporators. The sanction of the state is required.[29] It can only be created by or under legislative enactment.

Fourth, a partnership, by agreement of the partners, may do anything which is not unlawful.

[28] 1 Bl. Comm. 467-8.   [29] *Stowe* v. *Flagg*, 72 Ill. 397.

WHEN AND WHY

If business in dry goods is dull, it may deal in unintoxicating wet goods for the time being, or *vice versa*. A corporation, on the other hand, is a creature of limited powers and of special capacity, and may not lawfully exercise any powers except those conferred upon it or those reasonably to be implied from the powers conferred as incidental thereto or consequential thereupon.[30]

Fifth, in the case of a partnership there exists unlimited liability, by which I mean that a partner is liable to the last dollar of his personal fortune to the full extent of the partnership's indebtedness. So, if the firm becomes insolvent, he may stand to lose every dollar he owns in the world. In the case of the corporation, the situation is the precise opposite. There exists limited liability unless otherwise provided by law. The stockholder in a corporation, whose shares are paid in, is not liable for the corporate indebtedness.[31] The debts

[30] *Attorney General* v. *Mersey Ry. Co., L. R.* (1907), 1 Ch. Div. 81; reversed, L. R. (1907), A. C. 415; *Jacksonville, etc. Ry. & Navigation Co.* v. *Hooper*, 160 U. S. 514; *People* v. *Campbell*, 144 N. Y. 166, 38 N. E. 990; see, also, article, "The Power of a Corporation to Acquire Its Own Stock," 24 Yale Law Journal, 177 (1915).

[31] *Elenkrieg* v. *Siebrecht*, 238 N. Y. 254, 261, *per* Crane, J.; *People* v. *Coleman*, 133 N. Y. 279; *Hibbs* v. *Brown*, 190 N. Y. 167, see opinions *per* Edward T. Bartlett, J. and Werner, J.

of the corporation are its debts, and only its. They are not the individual stockholder's debts, and his private fortune cannot be touched. All, therefore, the stockholder stands to lose is the amount which he has invested in the corporation, no more, no less. This attribute of limited liability, pursuant to which, as has been said by the Court of Appeals, "the individual liability of the members, as it would have existed at common law, is lost by their creation into a corporation," [32] and becomes, so to speak, drowned out and obliterated, is regarded by most persons as the greatest advantage of incorporation. Indeed, many immigrants doubtless possess full knowledge of this fact before coming within hailing distance of the Statue of Liberty. Whether the legislatures have not been unduly liberal in this respect, particularly in the case of one-man companies where dummies are used for incorporating purposes, is a very grave problem, far beyond the scope of this paper.

Sixth, and most important, a partnership is not regarded by the law as a legal personality separate from the partners. A partnership takes and transfers property in the names of the partners. It sues or is sued in their names. While the man

[32] *People* v. *Coleman*, *supra*, at p. 284, *per* Finch, J.

in the street may regard it as a personality separate
from the sum total of the partners, the law does not
so regard it. A corporation, on the other hand, in
the eye of the law, is a legal entity and artificial
personality entirely distinct and separate from the
members who compose it.[33] It is a distinct person
in the eye of the law, though, as I have said, this
is by process of fiction. As such, it is capable of
suing and being sued, of contracting, of acquiring,
owning and disposing of property, within the objects and limits of its creation, the same as a natural
person, and one may deal with it, respecting its
corporate rights and properties, the same as with
a human owner. This is because the law has seen
fit to endow it with a juridical personality independent of any or all of its stockholders. While
this is doubtless a fiction, as Mr. Justice Holmes
well says, the very essence of the fiction is that
we must act upon it as if it were true.

Let me illustrate. Chief Justice Taney, of
the Supreme Court of the United States, said in
an early case: "Whenever a corporation makes a

[33] Cyclopedia of Law of Corporations, Fletcher, p. 26, and
cases there cited. For particularly apt illustrations in New
York, see opinions of Miller, J., in *Palmer* v. *Ring*, 113 App.
Div. 643, 99 N. Y. Supp. 290, and of Cardozo, J., in *People
ex rel. Studebaker Corp.* v. *Gilchrist*, 244 N. Y. 114.

15

contract, it is the contract of the legal entity, of the artificial being created by the charter, and not the contract of the individual members." [34] Doubtless this is true. It would be true even in such a case as this: Corporation A makes a written contract with you. It breaches the contract. You sue corporation B, claiming "it is back of corporation A and owns most of its stock." Obviously you have wandered into the wrong lane. The stockholder is not liable.[35] Your remedy is against the company with which you contracted, corporation A.

Or, take another case. [36] A British statute forbade the registration of any vessel owned by foreigners "in whole or in part, directly or indirectly." A corporation was chartered by Great Britain. Most of its stockholders were foreigners. The corporation sought to compel the registry of its vessel. This was resisted on the ground that so many of the stockholders were not British. The

[34] *Bank of Augusta* v. *Earle*, 13 Pet. (U. S.) 519, 587; see, also, *Erickson* v. *Revere Elevator Co.*, 110 Minn. 443, 126 N. W. 130.

[35] *New York Air Brake Co.* v. *International Steam Pump Co.*, 64 Misc. Rep. 347, 120 N. Y. Supp. 683; *Demarest* v. *Flack*, 128 N. Y. 205; *Tilley* v. *Coykendall*, 172 N. Y. 587; *Stone* v. *Cleveland, etc., R. Co.*, 202 N. Y. 352.

[36] *Queen* v. *Arnaud*, 9 Q. B. (Adol. & El.) 806.

court held the vessel must be registered; that the British corporation, and it alone, was the owner of the vessel in legal contemplation, and was therefore entitled to register it. The court said: "In no legal sense are the individual members the owners."

Button v. *Hoffman*,[37] decided by the Supreme Court of Wisconsin, is a leading case. There the sole owner of all the shares of stock of a corporation brought an action of replevin to recover certain personal property which had been unlawfully taken from the corporation's possession. As the plaintiff in his testimony expressed it, "I bought all the stock, I own all the stock now, I became the absolute owner of the mill. It belonged at that time to the company, and I am the company." The Wisconsin court politely but firmly informed him of his error, saying: "The owner of all the capital stock of a corporation does not own its property or any of it, and does not himself become the corporation, as a natural person, to own its property and do its business in his own name. While the corporation exists he is a mere stockholder of it, and nothing else." And the fact that the owner of all the stock is another corporation, has been held to make no difference in principle, since title to corporate property is in the corporate personality, and not in its stockholders, whether individual or corporate.

It was upon this theory that the Court of Appeals of this state held, in the celebrated case of *Werner* v. *Hearst*,[38] that Mr. Hearst was not liable individually for injuries sustained by a woman occasioned through the negligent conduct of the driver of a delivery truck owned by a newspaper corporation of which he was substantially the sole stockholder. Such a decision is entirely correct, because, if the corporation has been validly organized in its inception, the use of the corporation to prevent the incurring of personal obligations in the future is entirely proper and legitimate.[39] The policy of our law to-day sanctions incorporation with the consequent immunity from individual liability. It follows that no fraud is committed in incorporating for the precise purpose of avoiding and escaping personal responsibility. Indeed, that is exactly why most people incorporate, and those dealing with corporations know, or at least are presumed to know, the law in this regard. As to the policy of the law, I make no comment one way

[38] 177 N. Y. 63, 69 N. E. 221.
[39] 17 Columbia Law Review, at p. 141.

18

or the other. That is a matter for our omniscient legislators, not for judges and lawyers.

In the case of *New York Air Brake Co.* v. *International Steam Pump Co.*,[40] the capital stock of two manufacturing companies was owned by a third company. They had common officers and common offices, and acted through a common agent. X made a contract with the two former companies. He claimed that it was broken, and brought suit against all three companies as defendants. It was held that this could not be done, and that he could only sue the two former companies for the breach of the contracts made in their corporate names. The court pointed out that, where the capital stock of two manufacturing corporations is owned by a third, the latter is not liable for breach of contract by one of the former corporations, any more than any other stockholder would be, and that redress must be sought by plaintiff "by pursuing the particular corporation with which it contracted."

In the well-known English case of *Gramophone and Typewriter, Ltd.*, v. *Stanley*,[41] an English corporation owned all the stock of a German company, and it was contended that by reason of this fact

[40] 64 Misc. Rep. 347, 120 N. Y. Supp. 683, *per* Greenbaum, J.
[41] L. R. (1906), 2 K. B. 856, aff'd, L. R. (1908), 2 K. B. 89.

the business of the German company was the business of the English company, and that therefore the profits of the German company were profits really earned by the English company and could be taxed to the English company. Both the lower court and the Court of Appeals held that this could not be done and that the corporations must be regarded as distinct and separate.

An almost identical recent decision in the Court of Appeals of this state is *People ex rel. Studebaker Corp.* v. *Gilchrist.*[42] In this case the present Chief Judge [43] said: "Before 'the corporation *persona*' may be ignored, the evidence must show that 'the subsidiary is not left with any autonomy,' (Learned Hand, J., in *Procter & Gamble Co.* v. *Newton*, 289 Fed. 1013), and that the parent though in form speaking and acting through another, is operating the business directly for itself."

. The very recent case of *Berkey* v. *Third Avenue Ry. Co.*,[44] has aroused widespread discussion. In that case, the plaintiff was injured while riding on a car of the 42d Street Ry. Co., and, recognizing the inability of that company to pay a judgment, sued the Third Avenue Ry. Co., of which the 42d Street Ry. Co. was a subsidiary, claiming that the

[42] 244 N. Y. 114.   [43] *Ibid.*, at p. 123.   [44] 244 N. Y. 84.

corporate entity of the servient corporation should be disregarded, since it was the *alter ego* of the parent corporation, which owned its entire stock.

In his learned opinion, Cardozo, Ch. J., points out [45] that "substantially all the stock of that company is owned by the Third Avenue Ry. Co.," and the president of the Third Avenue Ry. Co., in making its report to the stockholders of the Third Avenue Ry. Co., exhibited the consolidated income of both companies in one statement.[46] "The members of the two boards of directors were nearly, though not quite, the same. Each road had the same executive officers, *i. e.*, the same president, treasurer, general manager, paymaster and counsel. The parent has made loans to the subsidiary from time to time, sometimes for construction, sometimes for operating expenses." [47] "All the cars, wherever used, are marked 'Third Avenue System.'" [48] "The cars when new ones become necessary, are bought by the defendant, and then leased to the subsidiaries, including, of course, the 42d Street Ry. Co., for a daily rental which is paid." [49]

[45] 244 N. Y., at p. 87.   [47] *Ibid.*, at p. 88.
[46] *Ibid.*, at p. 88.   [48] *Ibid.*, at p. 89.
[49] *Ibid.*, at p. 89.

DISREGARD OF CORPORATE FICTION—

The Court of Appeals held that, in spite of these facts, the 42d Street Ry. Co. was not a mere dummy or *alter ego* of the parent corporation, and in spite of the use of one company's assets by the other and the general interchangeable names that were used, the parent company could not be held legally liable for the torts of the subsidiary. Cardozo, Ch. J., said: [50] "In such circumstances, we thwart the public policy of the State instead of defending or upholding it, when we ignore the separation between subsidiary and parent, and treat the two as one."

The First Appellate Division had reversed [51] a judgment of dismissal on the theory that a question of fact existed as to whether or not the corporations were not in fact one and the same. The Court of Appeals reversed the Appellate Division and held, as matter of law, that they were not one and the same.

A powerful dissenting opinion was written by Crane, J., in which Pound, J., concurred, proceeding upon the theory that where one corporation actually controls another and operates both as a single system, the dominant company should be

[50] 244 N. Y., at p. 95.
[51] 217 App. Div. 504, *per* McAvoy, J.

held liable for injuries due to the negligence of the
subsidiary company. And the learned judge remarked that while separate bookkeeping entries
were made, "these things cannot hide the reality
or cover up the fact that the Third Avenue Ry.
Co., in operation, in control, in dominance, in execution and in the furnishing of service to the city of
New York, was the 42d Street Ry. Co." [52]

The case is indeed a close one. It is the sworn
duty of a court to decide what the law is, not what
abstract justice may be. Of the decision it might
be stated: "The victim is offered up to the gods
of jurisprudence on the altar of regularity." [53]
Yet some of the judges constituting the majority of
the bench in this case, have on other occasions acted
as veritable Samsons in bursting the green withes
of strict legal prescription. "The law must be
stable, and yet it cannot stand still." [54] Here is
one of the difficulties which faces us.

As I have said, there can be no doubt that in
general a corporation must be viewed as a personality, separate and distinct from its stockholders,
whether individual or corporate, but this fiction,

[52] 244 N. Y., at p. 102, *per* Crane, J.
[53] Cardozo, The Growth of the Law, p. 66.
[54] Pound, Interpretations of Legal History, p. 1; Cardozo,
The Growth of the Law, p. 2.

DISREGARD OF CORPORATE FICTION—

like every other fiction, must be employed with common sense and applied so as to promote the ends of justice. It must not be converted into a fetish. It must not be worshipped in the way savages worship a red cow or an ornamental totem pole as a supposed incarnation of a sacred spirit. There is always danger, when a fiction (whether corporate or otherwise) becomes so deeply rooted in the case law, that judges no longer remember its object and purpose, and apply the fiction to an extent where they refuse to consider and to penetrate into the actual facts behind it. Let me again illustrate.

In a case decided by the Supreme Court of Alabama,[55] A, B and C sold their business to X. They received the consideration. They agreed as a part of the transaction not to run a similar business in the town. A few months later they formed a corporation and immediately proceeded to engage in the same business. X sought an injunction. The learned court held that A, B and C were innocent because, forsooth, *they* were doing no wrong; that it was the corporation, and *it* alone, which

[55] *Moore & Handley Hardware Co.* v. *Towers Hardware Co.*, 87 Ala. 206, 6 Southern Rep. 41; see, also, article, "The Development of the Law," 23 Columbia Law Review, at pp. 705–6.

was carrying on the business,—and not the individuals A, B and C. A, B and C were thus allowed by a court of equity to circumvent and evade their solemn covenant for which they had received valuable consideration. The policy of the law as administered in progressive courts is to regard substance and to disregard form.[56] It is true that substance must not be treated as form or swept aside as technicality merely because that procedure may appear convenient in a certain case. It is, however, an entire misapplication of the corporate fiction to refuse an injunction in a case of this character. The corporation was used by A, B and C as a form of fraud, as a cloak for wrong, as a shield behind which they sought to evade a written contract obligation. The old maxim reads: *Qui facit per alium facit per se.* As I said fifteen years ago, in an article entitled "Piercing the Veil of Corporate Entity," [57] "The voices of the Sirens

[56] *Continental Tyre & Rubber Co.* v. *Daimler Co. Ltd.*, L. R. (1915), 1 K. B. 893, *per* Lord Reading, C. J.; reversed upon another proposition on appeal, *Daimler Co., Ltd.,* v. *Continental Tyre & Rubber Co.*, L. R. (1916), 2 A. C. 307.

[57] 12 Columbia Law Review 496 (June, 1912); cited, *Ross* v. *Jacobowitz*, 216 App. Div. 184, 187, 214 N. Y. Supp. 514, 517; *Farmers' Loan & Trust Co.* v. *Pierson*, 130 Misc. Rep. 110, 117, 222 N. Y. Supp. 532, 541; see, also, note, Yale Law Journal, vol. 36, 254–60 (Dec., 1926).

are at hand to decoy all but the most wary," and "there is no magic in incorporation." A, B and C were the same pack of thievish wolves, whether clad in the garments of fictitious corporate personality or in their own soiled furry coats. To allow the doctrine of the corporate fiction to prevent the doing of justice in such a case, converts courts into a public laughing-stock. Decisions of this type make the man in the street, as well as that *rara avis*,—the liberal lawyer,—impatient. [58] Should not the court have shaken aside fiction, form and phantom, in order to do justice? There is no compulsion to legal blindness. A decision refusing an injunction in a case of this type is contrary to the very genius and essence of the corporate fiction, and permits it to be used for ends and for purposes entirely subversive of its reason and policy.

A Virginia case creates equal doubts. In *People's Pleasure Park Co.* v. *Rohleder*,[59] a large tract of land was divided up into a number of lots, each deed of a lot containing a covenant providing that title to the real estate should never pass into

[58] Note, 36 Yale Law Journal, 254–60 (Dec., 1926); see editorials, New York Law Journal, Dec. 31, 1926, Aug. 16, 1926, and April 28, 1926; see, also, *Garrigues* v. *International Agricultural Corp.*, 159 App. Div. 877, 880, *per* Dowling, J.

[59] 109 Va. 439, 61 S. E. 794, 63 S. E. 981.

a person or persons of African descent or into a
colored person or persons. Thereafter, a corporation was organized "composed exclusively of negroes." It took title to a number of the lots and
proposed to establish an elaborate amusement
park for colored people. The corporation knew,
when it purchased the land, of the title restriction.
Suit was brought in equity by an owner of other
lots adjoining to have the deed to the corporation
cancelled and set aside. The court rendered judgment for the corporation, holding that though all
its members were negroes, yet the corporation was a
legal personality entirely separate, apart and distinct from its stockholders, and that therefore the
covenant was not breached. The court said, in
effect, that the corporation was not colored, because it "is a person which exists in contemplation
of law only, and not physically."

The decision entirely overlooks that the sole purpose of organization of the corporation was obviously
to evade and circumvent the title restriction forbidding negroes from taking the land. The fiction
should not have been applied.[60]

Suppose, again, that a corporation is organized for
the purpose of the commission of a fraud on creditors.

[60] Wormser, Private Corporations, pp. 13-14.

In *Booth* v. *Bunce*,[61] the members of a financially embarrassed partnership formed a corporation and then transferred to it the property of the partnership. X was a creditor of the partnership, Y, of the corporation. The issue before the court was in substance a contest between them to secure their respective claims out of certain personal property transferred by the partnership to the corporation. The Court of Appeals held that the property transferred might be taken on execution by X, the partnership creditor, since it appeared that the corporation was formed in bad faith and with the intent to defraud creditors. The court recognized that the corporate fiction could not be employed successfully for such purposes, declaring: "Deeds, obligations, contracts, judgments and *even corporate bodies* may be the instruments through which parties may obtain the most unrighteous advantages. All such devices and instruments have been resorted to, to cover up fraud, but whenever the law is invoked all such instruments are declared nullities; they are a perfect dead letter; the law looks upon them, as if they had never been executed." Whatever other explanations may be given by lawyers astute to cover up corporate fraud and wrongdoing, the fact

[61] 33 N. Y. 139.

WHEN AND WHY

remains that in cases of this sort, such outstanding
tribunals as the Court of Appeals of this state, and
the Supreme Court of Ohio in the well-known
Trebein case,[62] have refused to convert the doctrine
of fictitious corporate personality into a *reductio ad
absurdum.*[63]

The correct point of view seems to be this. In
ordinary, everyday business transactions, such as
the acquisition of property, the transfer of property,
the making of contracts, the institution and the
defense of suits, and the like, it is essential that the
distinction between the corporation as a legal entity
and a fictitious personality, on the one hand, and its
stockholders and officers, on the other hand, should
be strictly maintained. But, "where the corporate
form is used by individuals for the purpose of evading
the law, or for the perpetration of fraud, the courts
will not permit the legal entity to be interposed so
as to defeat justice." [64] In the latter class of cases,

[62] *First National Bank of Chicago* v. *Trebein Co.*, 59 Oh.
St. 316; see, also, article, 12 Columbia Law Review, at pp.
498–502.

[63] See Wormser, "Piercing the Veil of Corporate Entity,"
12 Columbia Law Review, 496; Hogg, "Personal Character
of a Corporation," 33 Law Quarterly R view, 76; Hohfeld,
"Fundamental Legal Conceptions, pp. 198–200 *et seq.;* note,
36 Yale Law Journal, 254–60 (Dec., 1926), and cases cited.

[64] *Erickson* v. *Revere Elevator Co.*, 110 Minn. 443, 126 N. W.

DISREGARD OF CORPORATE FICTION—

the courts will pierce the veil of corporate entity, though of course this phrase must not be taken literally, but, as a learned justice, commenting upon my use of it, has wisely and correctly said, it is simply designed as an "attractive and metaphorical designation for a digest of and commentary upon selected cases," [65] and is useful simply as a metaphor or figure of speech.

Let me give two further illustrations. First, one from the Supreme Court of Illinois in *Donovan* v. *Purtell*.[66] An unscrupulous real estate operator organized a number of "dummy " (the exact language of the court) realty companies. They all had their offices in the same room. They all had substantially the same officers and directors. The main purpose of their creation was to keep the various pieces of property owned by the operator out of judgment. What he would do was, to quote the court: "He would get up another company and put the property in the name of the new company, in order that it could be transferred, so that there would be no judgment against it; that he used the

130; *State* v. *Creamery Package Mfg. Co.*, 110 Minn. 415, 126 N. W. 126, and cases cited.

[65] *Farmers' Loan & Trust Co.* v. *Pierson*, 130 Misc. 110, 116-7, 222 N. Y. Supp., at p. 541.

[66] 216 Ill. 629, 75 N. E. 334.

property of the companies indiscriminately." The plain substance of the matter was that the so-called corporations in fact were the real estate operator under different flimsy cloaks. The fiction of separate corporate personality was being perverted. The learned court correctly held that a woman who had dealt with one of these corporations could hold the operator personally liable, saying: "A corporation is often organized to act as a 'cloak' for frauds. Such cases as these are becoming common, and the courts are becoming more and more inclined to ignore the corporate existence (by which, of course, the court meant the corporate fiction), when necessary, in order to circumvent the fraud." [67]

This case squarely holds that the corporate fiction cannot be employed as a cover for fraud. There is a much similar decision in this state, *Quaid* v. *Ratkowsky*,[68] wherein the Appellate Division in this Department was unanimously sustained by the Court of Appeals.[69]

The other case to which I would refer is the decision of the Supreme Court of the United States in the now celebrated case of *United States* v. *Lehigh*

[67] Cook, Corporations, 5th ed., § 663; see, also, *Lachman* v. *Martin*, 139 Ill. 450.

[68] 183 App. Div. 428, 170 N. Y. Supp. 812.

[69] 224 N. Y. 624, 121 N. E. 887.

DISREGARD OF CORPORATE FICTION—

Valley R. R. Co.[70] The so-called "commodities clause " of the Hepburn Act, provides: "It shall be unlawful for any railroad company to transport from any state * * * to any other state * * * any article manufactured, mined, or produced by it, or under its authority, or which it may own in whole or in part, or in which it may have any interest, direct or indirect." The Government, in its first proceeding, merely alleged that the Lehigh Valley R. R. Co. owned shares of stock in a coal company whose coal it was carrying. The court held that this did not establish a violation of the statute; that the mere fact that the railroad company may have held some stock in the coal company made no legal difference one way or the other. The Government then presented an amended complaint, in which it was set forth not only that the railroad company owned substantially all of the stock in the coal company, whose coal it was carrying, but also that the railroad company was using the coal company merely as a dummy and a device in order to evade the provisions of the Act, and that the railroad company had such complete power and domination over the affairs of the coal company that the

[70] 220 U. S. 257; see, also, *U. S.* v. *Delaware & Hudson Co.*, 213 U. S. 366.

coal company was in effect merely a department of the railroad. The Supreme Court, speaking through the late Mr. Chief Justice White, held that no such evasion could succeed, and, disregarding the corporate fiction and looking at the substance and reality of the situation, issued an injunction. The court thus held, for all practical purposes, that the railroad company was carrying its own coal and disregarded the fact that there were two separate juridical corporate fictions, because, to quote the learned court's own language, "ultimately considered they were but one and the same." In other words, where a corporation is so organized and its affairs are so conducted as to make it a mere instrumentality or an adjunct of another corporation, which, however, was not sufficiently established to the satisfaction of the court in the *Berkey* case,[71] its separate existence as a fictitious legal personality will be ignored.[72]

[71] 244 N. Y. 84; see, also, note, 12 Cornell Law Quarterly, 504-9 (June, 1927), and cases there cited; Ballantine, "Parent and Subsidiary Corporations," 14 Calif. Law Review, 12, 100 Central Law Journal, 107-12.

[72] *U. S.* v. *Lehigh Valley R. R. Co., supra; Quaid* v. *Ratkowsky, supra; U. S.* v. *Milwaukee Refrigerator Transit Co.,* 142 Fed. 247; *Linn & Lane Timber Co.* v. *United States,* 236 U. S. 574; *Interstate Telegraph Co.* v. *Baltimore & Ohio Telegraph Co.,* 51 Fed. 49, aff'd, 54 Fed. 50; Re Muncie Pulp Co.,

DISREGARD OF CORPORATE FICTION—

Shakespeare says, in his "Comedy of Errors," Act V, Scene 1:

"Duke. One of these men is Genius to the other; and so of these:
"Which is the natural man, and which the spirit? Who deciphers them?
"Dromio of Syracuse. I, sir, am Dromio; command him away.
"Dromio of Ephesus. I, sir, am Dromio; pray let me stay."

If the proof is sufficiently strong, the law may and will strip aside the mask and fiction, and look to and "decipher" the actual facts behind them. How can the mere process of duplicate christening create distinct juridical personalities in such cases? How can the law treat such corporate Dromios as other than one and the same, unless it would be pilloried in the stocks of good horse sense? Our jurisprudence must be practical. The law is a practical science, not a game or a contest of wits. A corporation, for

139 Fed. 546, 71 C. C. A. 530; *In re Rieger, Kapner & Altmark,* 157 Fed. 609; *Gay* v. *Hudson River Elec. P. Co.,* 187 Fed. 12, 15, 109 C. C. A. 66; *Hunter* v. *Baker Motor Vehicle Co.,* 225 Fed. 1006; see, also, dissenting opinion of Crane, J., concurred in by Pound, J., in *Riley* v. *Pierce Oil Corp.,* 245 N. Y. 152, at pp. 154–6; also *Davis* v. *Alexander,* 269 U. S. 114; *Chicago, Milwaukee & St. Paul Ry. Co.* v. *Minn. Civic Ass'n,* 247 U. S. 490, 500–1.

34

purposes of cases of this type, must be looked upon like an expansible symbol. For instance, a bracket like $[A^2 - B^2]$ in an algebraic expression; which, while treated as a unit for most purposes, is nevertheless capable at any time of being expanded to show its real constituency.[73] In the *Lehigh Valley* case, when the facts are closely scrutinized, we see the justification for the learned court's statement that a statute cannot be evaded by any such fictitious device. Fat corporation fees inspire corporation lawyers as catnip inspires cats. But their devices cannot defeat the law if it is honestly, intelligently, and, above all, fearlessly, administered.

Now, of course, it is often extremely difficult to draw the line. Whether the majority or minority judges in cases as close as the *Berkey* case are correct is a problem upon which reasonable men may reasonably differ. So long as the courts recognize the general principle that the corporate fiction must not be employed so as to defeat the end for which it was invented, it does not make such vast difference how any particular case is decided, for out of the facts the law arises, and on factual situations judges will always differ.

"The answer, perhaps, is," to quote the words of

[73] 2 Fordham Law Review, p. 24.

Mr. Justice Chitty,[74] "that courts of justice ought
not to be puzzled by such old scholastic questions
as to where a horse's tail begins and where it ceases.
You are obliged to say, 'this is a horse's tail,' at
some time." It is serviceable to bear in mind that
"the purpose in making all corporations is the
accomplishment of some public good," and that no
rule of law, logic or common sense requires courts
to employ or apply the fiction of corporate personality as a whitewash for corporate wrongdoing.
The power of courts to frustrate the wrongful devices of astute attorneys should be at least coextensive with the distorted ingenuity which devises
them. The lawyers who organize corporations
not to disentangle human affairs but to entan-
gle them, remind one of the lines of poetry written in relation to the fact that one of the streets
in the London Strand abutting on the river
Thames is tenanted by lawyers, and which read as
follows:

"At the top of my street the lawyers abound,
    And down at the bottom the barges are found;
    Fly, honesty, fly to some safer retreat,
    There's craft in the river and craft in the street."

[74] *Lavery* v. *Purssell* (1888), 57 L. J. Ch. 570, 574, 39 Ch.
Div. 508.

WHEN AND WHY

The courts, to their credit, are daily demonstrating their ability to cope with such exercises of perverted legal skill. The Supreme Court of the United States, in particular, has never allowed the fiction to stand in the way either of circumventing fraud or administering justice, and, as Mr. Justice Holmes put it in his letter to me, carefully guards against the fiction "becoming a non-conductor in the wrong place." Or, as the court itself stated it, in a recent case,[75] "A growing tendency is therefore exhibited in the courts to look beyond the corporate form to the purpose of it and to the officers who are identified with that purpose." In other words, they look "to see the man behind." [76] Or, if it is preferable to use a metaphor, they pierce the veil of corporate entity.[77]

Would legislation be of any avail? Could the law of corporations be "restated" or "codified" so as to formulate a series of propositions which could be automatically applied? In my judgment this is

[75] *McCaskill Co.* v. *United States*, 216 U. S. 504, 514; *Simmons Creek Coal Co.* v. *Doran*, 142 U. S. 417; see, also, *Quaid* v. *Ratkowsky, supra*, and cases there cited.

[76] Mr. Justice Holmes, in *Donnell* v. *Herring-Hall-Marvin Safe Co.*, 208 U. S. 267, 273.

[77] *Farmers' Loan & Trust Co.* v. *Pierson, supra*, citing article, 12 Columbia Law Review, 496.

not only impossible but preposterous.[78] Human life and relations in regard to corporate development are far too complex to permit of any such formulation. The law is a growth and must not be shackled. Corporate law, in particular, develops so rapidly that such a formulation would be stale even before the date of its publication. The law moves. It must be moulded carefully to meet the ever changing needs of the present hour. It must not be placed in a strait-jacket. Those who would codify it fail to understand the spirit and genius which underlie it. Law is simply a part of life itself, and just as life grows, develops and progresses, so, also, with the law. It is a practical science. It must be dealt with in a practical spirit, by practical men, in a practical way. The best way to handle the problem is through the orderly and timely development and evolution of the common law pursuant to the established judicial methods and legal processes of over a thousand years. May we be preserved from statutory interference!

Only the other day the chairman of the committee to revise and codify the corporation laws of a midwestern state wrote me for a copy of this paper,

[78] "The Development of the Law," 23 Columbia Law Review, at pp. 713–4, and authorities there cited.

which he felt would aid in the formulation of the new corporate theorems to be propounded. I felt tempted to write him, in reply, a little verse which used to be popular when I was a boy:

> "I thank my God the sun and moon
> Are both stuck up so high
> That no presumptuous hand can stretch
> And pluck them from the sky.
> If they were not, I do believe
> That some reforming ass
> Would recommend to take them down
> And light the world with gas."

What we need are not more statutes. There are already too many of them. Statute making, even ahead of bootlegging, is the chief American occupation. The law should be allowed to develop as a slow, steady growth, sloughing off bad precedents from time to time and making new ones to meet the demands of a developing human society. Too numerous statutes are subversive of the very spirit and theory of our system of law.

In conclusion, some of you may ask, can any general rule be laid down? Fifteen years ago I asked myself this question, and in the Columbia Law Review [79] I endeavored to answer it. To-day

---

[79] 12 Columbia Law Review, 496, at pp. 517-8.

DISREGARD OF CORPORATE FICTION—

I am older and less wise—far less wise. I have learned to realize that the formulation of legal propositions which can be applied with meticulous exactitude is a highly dangerous undertaking. You cannot bind up legal principles with baby blue ribbon in orderly little parcels and label them "thus and thus" or "so and so." The most one can do is to state, in the most general way, that, in the present condition of the authorities, a corporation will be looked upon by the courts as a legal personality, for ordinary purposes in everyday business transactions, as a general principle and until adequate reason to the contrary appears; but that the fiction will be disregarded and the law will look to see the men and facts behind the fiction whenever it is employed "to defraud creditors, to evade an existing obligation, to circumvent a statute, to achieve or perpetuate monopoly, or to protect knavery and crime." [80]

Our Lady of the Common Law is garbed beautifully. I see her before me, clad in radiant robes of purest white. I see her gown besprinkled with pearls and diamonds. I see a starry halo above her head. She walks majestically and with a stately mien. Her task is to furnish us a code of justice as beautiful

[80] 12 Columbia Law Review, at p. 517.

and sublime as the vision of herself. But now, as I gaze, the picture alters. I see Our Lady wielding in her hand a bright sword. I see the sword flash. It has the thunders and the power of the Almighty behind it. It cuts down wrong. It stamps on fraud. It blots out vice and crime.

No cunning use of fiction can stand before that sword. It strikes down the subtle chicanery of the sharpest lawyer. It sees through every device of the most cleverly wrought evasion. It is not helpless against the mail of corporate cloaks, though moulded from the stoutest steel. The sword of justice can cut through to the heart and kernel. The time shall never arrive in the development of Our Lady's long and successful career when a fiction can be perverted in such manner that her sword shall be helpless to strike it down, nor will she ever permit sophism to be enthroned above law or trickery above justice.

Piercing the Veil of Corporate Entity [1]

PERHAPS no two authorities on the law of corporations are in complete accord as to the exact nature of the juristic concepts of corporate entity and corporate personality. Corporations have been regarded as " but associations of individuals, " [2] as artificial personalities,[3] as merely "the sum of legal relations" subsisting in respect to the corporate enterprise.[4] They have even been regarded as actual persons and dealt with in a quite anthropomorphic manner.[5] A brilliant writer has recently suggested that corporate entity is not imaginary or fictitious but quite real, whereas corporate personality is a fiction whose origin is to be found in the psychological tendency towards personification.[6]

[1] Columbia Law Review, Vol. 12 (1912).

[2] Lumpkin, J., in *Hightower* v. *Thornton* (1850), 8 Ga. 486, 492; *cf.* Morawetz, Private Corporations (2d ed.), Preface.

[3] Marshall, C. J., in *Dartmouth College* v. *Woodward* (U. S. 1819), 4 Wheat. 518, 636; *cf.* 1 Bl. Comm. 467–8.

[4] Taylor, Private Corporations (2d ed.), §§ 36, 51.

[5] Holzendorff's Rechtslexikon, art. Juristische Person: Prof. Gierke.

[6] Arthur W. Machen, Jr., 24 Harv. L. Rev. 253, 347.

OF CORPORATE ENTITY

It is not the present purpose of the writer to discuss these divers theories or to indulge in the tempting but profitless discussion—more metaphysical than legal—as to the true anatomy of the corporate concept. The difficult problem for the corporation lawyer of to-day is to learn how to employ the concept, to know when to apply fearlessly the theory of the existence of a corporation as an entity distinct and separate from its shareholders and when, on the other hand, just as fearlessly to disregard it. And the voices of the Sirens are at hand to decoy all but the most wary.

All writers on corporation law agree that in certain cases and at certain times a corporation is to be regarded as an entity quite separate and apart from the individual shareholders. Practically all writers agree, also, that in some cases this entity theory must be disregarded. Sometimes we look upon the corporation as a unit, at other times we look upon it as a collection of persons. When should the concept of corporate entity be adhered to, when should it be disregarded?

The concept is not an "open sesame," which will open all gates. When to use it, when to ignore it, is the present-day dilemma. The scope and purpose of this article are to seek to supply an answer and to indicate in what classes of cases the "entity concept" should be ignored; incidentally, to demonstrate how the courts, again and again, have frustrated each and every attempt to commit iniquity, to perpetrate fraud, to achieve monopoly, or to accomplish wrongs, under the guise, and hiding behind the veil, of corporate existence. The refusal of the courts to allow quiddits and quillets to stand in the way of justice is nowhere better exemplified.

It has been oftentimes stated that courts of law invariably adhere to the entity theory even though gross miscarriages of justice result. It is quite true that equity, less abashed by forms or fictions than a court of law, is more willing to draw aside the veil and look at the real parties in interest. However, courts of law have, again and again, refused to be trammeled by scholastic logic and mediæval corporate ideas, which frequently serve only to distort or hide the truth. This word of warning, therefore, at the outset: while equity more willingly and more frequently regards the corporation as a collection of persons than does a court of law, yet, as will be seen, the rule in courts of law is not unbending.

As early as 1809, it was perceived that in many cases the literal application of the notion that a corporation is only a legal entity, and nothing more,

OF CORPORATE ENTITY

would work injustice. The Supreme Court of the United States, from its genesis, had taken over the language of the year books, and, proclaiming its allegiance, had agreed with Coke that "a corporation aggregate of many is invisible, immortal, and rests only in intendment and consideration of the law." [7] Now, if a corporation is merely a legal entity, if it is clothed only with invisibility and intangibility, it could not, of course, be a citizen of a state. The federal constitution, however, in article three, section two, limits, *inter alia*, the jurisdiction of the federal courts "to controversies between *citizens* of different states." In 1809,[8] Chief Justice Marshall, therefore, in order to preserve the jurisdiction of the federal courts over corporations, was compelled to look beyond the entity "to the character of the individuals who compose the corporation." The court proclaimed that "substantially and essentially" the parties to the suit are the stockholders, and that of their several citizenships cognizance would be taken. It is not within the scope of this article to discuss the development and history of this now repudiated ruling. One theory of federal jurisdiction to-day is that a corporation

[7] 10 Co. Rep. 32 b; and see Co. Litt. 250 a.
[8] *Bank of United States* v. *Deveaux* (U. S. 1809), 5 Cranch 61.

is an association of persons, citizens,—fortified and
buttressed by an arbitrary legal fiction that these
persons are citizens of the state fathering the entity.[9]
The other theory regards a corporation "to all in-
tents and purposes as a person, although an artificial
person, * * * capable of being treated as a citizen
of that state, as much as a natural person." [10]

It is simply necessary for present purposes to note
that as early as 1809, the United States Supreme
Court did not regard it as reasonable that the operation of the concept should be permitted to oust the
federal courts of their important and far-reaching
jurisdiction over corporations, a result which any
overzealous adherence to the theory of corporate
entity would inevitably entail. Already at that day,
"courts have drawn aside the veil and looked at the
character of the individual corporators." [11]

The breach in the rampart had been made. The
mediæval bulwark had been stormed. Marshall's
decision, though later disregarded and overruled—in

[9] Grier, J., in *Marshall* v. *Baltimore & Ohio R. R. Co.* (U. S.
1853), 16 How. 314, 328–9; Shiras, J., in *St. L. & San F.
R. R. Co.* v. *James* (1896), 161 U. S. 545, 562.

[10] Wayne, J., in *Louisville, Cincinnati & Charleston R. R. Co.*
v. *Letson* (U. S. 1844), 2 How. 497, 558.

[11] Williams, C. J., in *Fairfield County Turnpike Co.* v.
Thorp (1839), 13 Conn. 173, 179, commenting on the decision
in *Bank of U. S.* v. *Deveaux, supra.*

fact, he himself is said to have indicated his impatience with it [12]—had served to indicate that a clearer perspective often followed where the web (or as Mr. Taylor would probably say, the cob-web) of corporate entity was fearlessly brushed aside.

An important and most illuminating line of cases where courts refuse to be tied down by the entity theory is seen in the numerous instances of judicial impatience with all attempts to hamper, delay or defraud creditors by means of "dummy" incorporations. In all such instances courts, whether of law, of equity or of bankruptcy, do not hesitate to penetrate the veil and to look beyond the juristic entity at the actual and substantial beneficiaries. The decision of the New York Court of Appeals in *Booth* v. *Bunce* [13] is one of the earliest in point. In that case the members of a financially embarrassed partnership united in forming a manufacturing corporation, under the general incorporation laws. They then transferred to it the property of the partnership. X was a *bona fide* creditor of the partnership; Y, of the corporation. The issue was, in substance, a contest between them to secure their

[12] Remarks of Wayne, J., in *Louisville, etc., R. R. Co.* v. *Letson, supra,* 555.

[13] (1865) 33 N. Y. 139.

respective claims out of certain personal property transferred by the partnership to the corporation. The court held that the property transferred might be taken on execution by X, since it appeared that the corporation was formed in bad faith and with the intent to defraud creditors.

The trial court charged the jury:

"they had to determine but one question, and that was, that if this corporation was fairly organized, and the sale of the property to it by Montgomery and Lund (the partners) was also fair and done without fraudulent intent, the defendants, (Y) were entitled to recover; if, on the contrary, the company was organized to defraud the creditors of Montgomery and Lund, and the property was transferred to them by Montgomery and Lund in furtherance of that fraudulent purpose, the plaintiff (X) was entitled to recover. * * * " [14]

This charge, on appeal, was upheld. The defendants, of course, invoked the sacred doctrine of corporate entity. They insisted that the court had no right to ignore that holy concept. The learned court, however, recognized that there was no magic in incorporation and, declaring that the vice of fraud contaminated anything,—even the device of incorporation,—held the entity for all practical purposes a nullity. The scheme was clever, but it did not

[14] (1865) 33 N. Y. at p. 156.

meet with success. The court, to its credit, was not afraid to lift the veil.

Be it noted that this case was in a court of *law*. The suit was in tort for conversion. Yet it was said:

" * * * Deeds, obligations, contracts, judgments, and *even corporate bodies* may be the instruments through which parties may obtain the most unrighteous advantages. All such devices and instruments have been resorted to, to cover up fraud, but whenever the *law* is invoked all such instruments are declared nullities; they are a perfect dead letter; the law looks upon them as if they had never been executed. * * * " [15]

In other words, courts of law do not tolerate any attempt to hinder, delay, or defraud creditors by means of a resort to "the veil of corporate entity." The ingenuity of the rogue, with his arsenal of scholastic sophistry, was met and overwhelmed by the sane and stern refusal to be bound by the entity theory.

In a recent bankruptcy case,[16] the receiver applied to extend his receivership to the property of a corporation which he alleged to be a mere *alter ego* of a bankrupt partnership. The members of the partnership firm owned 485 shares of the outstanding stock; the other five shares outstanding were owned by a close relative of one of the partners. Business

[15] (1865) 33 N. Y. at p. 157.
[16] In re Rieger, Kapner & Altmark (1907), 157 Fed. 609.

between the corporation and partnership was conducted in such manner that the state of accounts between them was impossible of ascertainment. The argument, of course, was made in behalf of the bankrupts and the corporation that the corporation "existed as a separate and distinct entity." The court brushed aside this contention and declared that the doctrine of corporate entity is "not so sacred" that courts, looking through shams and forms to the actual substance of things, may not ignore the concept in order to preserve the rights of innocent parties or to circumvent fraud. The corporation, it was pointed out, was organized merely to give these disingenuous individuals a double line of credit and to hinder and delay their creditors in the event of insolvency. There was no hesitation. There were no qualms. The court, penetrating the subterfuge, subjected the entire property, both that of the corporation and of the partnership, to the claims of creditors. Hands may be held up in horror at the circumstance that five shares of the corporate stock were not owned by members of the partnership. The court held, and quite correctly, that this was quite immaterial under the glaring circumstances of the case. The decision is submitted to be sound. The corporate organization was but an *alter ego*

OF CORPORATE ENTITY

of the partnership. It was the same pack of thievish
wolves, whether in the "entity" garments of little
Red Riding Hood's grandmother or in their own
furry coats. One was subsidiary and auxiliary to
the other. To allow the doctrine of corporate entity
to intervene would be to convert a court of justice
into a public laughing-stock.

Another illustrative decision is *Hibernia Insurance Company* v. *St. Louis & New Orleans Trans.
Co.*[17] That case arose in *equity* and it was held that
chancery would not permit the stockholders in one
corporation to organize another and transfer all the
corporate property of the former to the latter, without paying all the corporate debts. It was further
held that, where such a transfer is made, the obligations of the old corporation may be enforced against
the new corporation to the full extent of the assets
received. Again, we see the concept of corporate
entity ignored. Is not the decision reasonable?
After all, looking at the real and substantial parties
in interest—the bone and muscle men and women
shareholders,—is it not clear that all they did was to
change their habiliments? Is it not reasonable to
hold, as the court did, that they could not by the
device of incorporation shield their property from the

[17] (1882) 13 Fed. 516.

51

payment of their just debts? Would a contrary decision not amount to judicial exaltation of a stumbling block? Would it not be a mockery to hold otherwise? Is not the court justified in shaking aside form and phantom in order to get at the substance?

In *Montgomery Web Company* v. *Dienelt*,[18] the situation was quite similar to that in the preceding case. The suit was by a creditor of one company to set aside a conveyance by it to another, as in fraud of his rights. It appeared that the latter company was formed substantially by the shareholders of the former, who gave up their stock in it for stock in the latter, this being substantially all the consideration given. This was unanimously held to be a fraud upon the creditors of the former company. The court said:

" * * * The only real difficulty in the present case is whether the stockholders are so completely severed, in the view of the law, from the corporation behind which they hide, as to prevent a creditor from asserting their identity in fact, for the purpose of securing payment out of property which was theirs under one name, and is still theirs under another. Is the Montgomery Company so completely a new and different person from the Aronia company that the law must

[18] (1890) 133 Pa. St. 585.

close its eyes to the fact that the difference is a mere juggle of names? *We do not think there is any compulsion to such legal blindness.* * * * " [19]

One other case will serve to make it clear that the courts ignore the concept of legal corporate entity when used as a shield for fraudulent attempts to swindle creditors. In *First National Bank of Chicago* v. *Trebein Company*,[20] an insolvent individual, one F. C. Trebein, together with his wife, his daughter, his son-in-law, and his brother-in-law, formed a corporation and then conveyed to it every vestige of tangible property which he owned. His creditors insisted and proved that the purpose in creating the corporation was to hinder and defraud them. The court held that "the corporation was in substance another F. C. Trebein," and that "his identity as owner of the property was no more changed by his conveyance to the company than it would have been by taking off one coat and putting on another." It was held to be immaterial that four out of five hundred shares of stock were held not by Trebein himself but by his relatives; that circumstance quite properly did not deter the Supreme Court of Ohio from deciding that the corporation was "in substance another F. C. Trebein."

[19] (1890) 133 Pa. St. at p. 595.   [20] (1898) 59 Oh. St. 316.

PIERCING THE VEIL

Even the over-fervent adherent of the orthodox entity theory must concede that these decisions ignore the concept, and very justly. To give further instances would be to reiterate without need.[21]

Closely related to the preceding group of cases are the already numerous and constantly increasing number of decisions which hold that, where a corporation is so organized and controlled and its affairs are so conducted as to make it a mere instrumentality or agent or adjunct of another corporation, its separate existence as a distinct corporate entity will be ignored, and the two corporations will be regarded in legal contemplation as one unit. A striking illustration—perhaps the most notable—is the Federal decision, *In Re Muncie Pulp Company*.[22] In that case, the Pulp Company caused the incorporation and organization of the Great Western Natural Gas Company and the transfer to it of its gas and oil wells and lands. The president and treasurer of the pulp company owned every share

[21] See, also, *Donovan* v. *Purtell* (1905), 216 Ill. 629; *Kellogg* v. *Douglas County Bank* (1897), 58 Kan. 43; *Bremen Saving Bank* v. *Branch, etc., Co.* (1891), 104 Mo. 425; *Lusk* v. *Riggs* (1902), 65 Neb. 258, 262; *Terhune* v. *Hackensack Savings Bank* (1889), 45 N. J. Eq. 344; *Andres* v. *Morgan* (1900), 62 Oh. St. 236; *Bennett* v. *Minott* (1896), 28 Ore. 339; *Vance* v. *McNabb Coal, etc., Co.* (1892), 92 Tenn. 47; *Accord*.

[22] (1905) 139 Fed. 546; 71 C. C. A. 530.

of stock of the Great Western Company, save one share which was held by a third person in order to have a resident director in Indiana, the state of incorporation. The Great Western Company kept no separate books, its affairs were managed by the Pulp Company, and it was treated as an agent of the Pulp Company for all purposes. Subsequently the Pulp Company went into bankruptcy. The receiver demanded the delivery to him of the property of the Great Western Company as a part of the assets of the Pulp Company, and was refused. The court sustained the receiver, and held that the Great Western Company was merely the dummy of the bankrupt Pulp Corporation, and that its property belonged in law to the bankrupt. In his opinion, Coxe, Circuit Judge, said:

"The Great Western Company was undoubtedly a mere creature of the pulp company, having no independent business existence, and organized solely for the purpose of facilitating the business of the latter. The Great Western Company has no shadow of claim to the property in controversy, and to permit it, or its president, or shareholders, to dispose of such property, is to sanction a fraud upon the creditors of the pulp company. * * *" [23]

It is not enough, however, that shareholders in two corporations are identical. It is not enough

[23] (1905) 139 Fed. at p. 548.

that one owns shares in the other. It is not enough that they have mutual interrelated dealings. In order to disregard the entity it must clearly appear that one corporation is but the "business conduit" of the other.

Perhaps in no manner can these propositions involved be more clearly illustrated than by contrasting the actual decisions. To illustrate: In *Interstate Telegraph Company* v. *Baltimore and Ohio Telegraph Company*,[24] it appeared that a railroad corporation caused a telegraph company to be incorporated, became the sole owner of its stock, elected its own officers and employees as officers thereof, and held out such company as authorized to contract for its whole railway telegraph system. It was held that the railway company was, in truth, the owner of the telegraph company, and that the latter company was a mere department, or bureau, of the railroad company, only created and maintained for the railway company's benefit as an agent to make contracts. The inevitable corollary follows that, had the railroad corporation become insolvent during the existence of the telegraph company, the court would have treated the telegraph company's property as the property of the

[24] (1892) 51 Fed. 49, aff'd (1893) 54 Fed. 50.

56

railroad company,—notwithstanding the agonizing
pleas for separate corporate entity which undoubtedly would have been raised by astute counsel.

On the other hand, the recent case of *In re
Watertown Paper Company* [25] demonstrates how
hazy is the border-line and how supremely difficult
it is to determine when to tear aside the barrier
of distinct corporate existence and when to leave
it undisturbed. In that case, after the organization
of a paper company, its stockholders caused the organization of a pulp company, with funds advanced
by the paper company, but for the account of its
stockholders to whom the advancements were
charged. The paper company itself owned no
stock of the pulp company. While the two
corporations mingled their affairs, *e. g.*, the paper
company purchasing its pulp, supplies, etc., from
the pulp company, and the stockholders in control
apparently regarded the two corporations merely
as different departments of one general business,
yet separate corporate organizations were kept up,
distinct sets of corporate books were maintained,
and each conducted its own business in its own
name. The court held that the affairs of the two
corporations were not so conducted as to make one

[25] (1909) 169 Fed. 252.

company a mere dummy or instrumentality of the other and that the pulp company could enforce its claim against the bankrupt estate of the paper company. Noyes, Circuit Judge, recognized the rule laid down in the preceding cases but distinguished the case before him on the grounds, 1, that separate corporate organizations were kept up; 2, that each corporation had its own creditors, its own assets, and conducted business in its own name; 3, that separate books of account were kept. He seemingly regarded it as immaterial that at times the two corporations mingled their affairs and that lax business methods between them were plainly shown. The decision is marked by a tendency to stick somewhat overclosely to the entity theory. The learned judge conceded that it might be disregarded in order to circumvent fraud, or where one corporation, as in the *Muncie* case, *supra*, was but a separate name for the other. The *Watertown* case, however, he did not deem as coming within the exceptions, but rather within the rule that the distinct corporate existence of two separate, although associated, corporations will be upheld by the courts.

It cannot be too strongly emphasized that mere identity of stockholders *per se* does not operate to destroy the distinct corporate existence of two corporations. So much is clear.[26] It must further appear by clear and convincing evidence that the corporation created is only an adjunct of the business of its creator,—a mere agency, or instrumentality, through which it acts,—a mere business department, or bureau, so to speak. Once, however, these facts appear, a court, whether of law or equity or bankruptcy, should look through the thin guise of corporate entity to the actual substance of things and should not hesitate to cast aside the entity concept in order to achieve justice.

Where a corporation is organized as a mere sham or device in order to evade an existing legal obligation, recent decisions establish that the courts, even without regard to actual fraud, are wont to disregard the entity theory. There is perhaps no better illustration of this rule than the notable decision of the Supreme Court of California in *Higgins* v. *Cal. Petroleum & Asphalt Company, et al.*[27] A lessee corporation in that case, with intent to evade the payment of royalties under a lease, conveyed

[26] *Richmond & I. Construction Co.* v. *Richmond R. R. Co.* (1895), 68 Fed. 105, 108, 15 C. C. A. 289; *Lange* v. *Burke* (1901), 69 Ark. 85, 88; *Waycross Airline R. R. Co.* v. *Offerman & W. R. R. Co.* (1900), 109 Ga. 827; *N. Y. Airbrake Co.* v. *International Steam Pump Co.* (N. Y., 1909), 64 Misc. Rep. 347, 120 N. Y. Supp. 683, *per* Greenbaum, J.

[27] (1905) 147 Cal. 363.

title to a second corporation. The main, apparently
the sole, purpose of this organization was to evade
the obligations of the lease. Thereafter, the second
corporation conveyed to a third, seemingly with
the same end still in view. It appeared that each
of the three corporations had substantial identity.
Each had been formed by the same persons. They
"'had their offices together in the same room, had
practically the same officers and were organized by
the same persons and for substantially the same
purposes.'" The court did not find that there was
any actual fraud in the transaction. Without regard to actual fraud, however, in the formation of
each of the succeeding corporations and the transfer of title thereto, such transfer, as against the lessor holding an existing obligation against the original
lessee corporation, was held, nevertheless, "con-
structively fraudulent as a matter of law." The
court decreed that all of the corporations were
jointly liable for the royalties to the lessor, saying
that "the three corporations defendant are really
the same." [28] This decision—all the stronger because at law and not in equity—and those in harmony with it, are sound law. To allow the concept
of legal entity, attributed to a duly formed incor-

[28] (1905) 147 Cal. 363, at p. 368.

porated company, to stand as a stumbling block in the path leading to justice would be tantamount to allowing the greatest iniquity to be perpetrated under the concept as a shield. It would be contrary to the very genius of the concept itself to allow it to be used for ends and for purposes subversive of its reason.

Similarly in *Brundred* v. *Rice*,[29] the promoters of a corporation organized a separate entity for the purpose of consummating an illegal railway rebate agreement, thinking no doubt to shield themselves from consequences in that manner. They had the effrontery, *mirabile dictu*, even when all the facts were laid bare in open court, to claim that the interposition of a "legal entity" precluded their being held personally liable. It was held that "the act of incorporating can be of no avail to them as a defense." The court, penetrating the sham, rightly declared that there was nothing "sacred in a certificate of incorporation," and that their ingenious, tricky device was of no avail. Again, in this case, the proceedings were in a court of law, and not in equity. There was, however, not the slightest hesitation manifested in penetrating to the essential root and gist of things.

[29] (1892) 49 Oh. St. 640.

One further illustration will suffice. In *Donovan v. Purtell*,[30] a clever and unscrupulous real estate operator organized a number of different realty companies, all of which were so much "straw." They all had their offices in the same room, they all had substantially the same officers, and the main purpose of the organization of each was to keep the various properties owned by the operator out of judgment. As testified to by one witness,

"'* * * there were judgments against these different companies, and he (Donovan, the operator) would get up another company and put the property in the name of the new company, in order that it could be transferred, so that there would be no judgment against it.' That he used the property of the companies indiscriminately." [31]

The sum and substance of the whole matter was that the corporations, in point of fact, were really the real estate operator under different cloaks. It was held that an individual who had dealt with one of these corporations, as such, could hold the operator personally liable. As said by Mr. Justice Magruder, speaking for the Supreme Court of Illinois,

"* * * When appellant received appellee's money, he was not conducting business under a *bona fide* cor-

[30] (1905) 216 Ill. 629.　　　　[31] *Ibid.* 634.

porate organization, but was using a corporate entity for the transaction of his private business * * *." [32]

The court indicated its refusal to be trammeled by the theory of corporate entity and impatiently ignored the usual defense,—the "corporate concept"!

Oftentimes the corporate form of organization is adopted in an endeavor to evade a statute or to modify its intent. A forceful example is to be found in the learned decision of the United States Supreme Court disregarding the theory of corporate entity in enforcing the "commodities clause" of the Hepburn Act.[33] The commodities clause provides that

"It shall be unlawful for any railroad company to transport from any State * * * to any other State * * * any article * * * manufactured, mined or produced by it, or under its authority, or which it may own in whole or in part, or in which it may have any interest, direct or indirect * * *."

The government, in the first suit, alleged that the Lehigh Valley Railroad Company owned stock in a coal company whose goods it was carrying. On demurrer, it was held that no violation of the statute was thereby shown; the court interpreted "interest, direct or indirect " as meaning only a legal or equi-

[32] (1905) 216 Ill. at p. 641.

[33] *U. S.* v. *Lehigh Valley R. R. Co.* (1911), 220 U. S. 257, 31 Sup. Ct. 387 (*per* White, C. J.).

table interest in the transported articles.[34]   The
government, after this first and very serious blow,
presented an amended complaint in which it was
set forth, in addition to the allegations of the prior
complaint, that the railroad company was using
the coal company merely as a sham, a device
and a dummy, in order to evade the provisions
of the act.   The court held that no such evasion could succeed, and, disregarding the corporate
concept and looking at the substance and reality
of things, decided that it was within its jurisdiction
to issue an injunction.[35]   It is submitted that every
dictate of sound reason warranted the court in
holding as it did.

The late Justice Brewer in his notable concurring
opinion in *Northern Securities Company* v. *United
States*,[36] pointed out that, where a corporation was
organized merely as a convenient means of combining separate railroad properties under one control
the court could shake aside the veil of entity and regard the combination as just "as direct a restraint
of trade by destroying competition as the appoint-
ment of a committee to regulate rates."   In other

[34] *U. S.* v. *Delaware & Hudson Co.* (1909), 213 U. S. 366,
esp. 413.

[35] (1911) 220 U. S. 257 *et seq.*

[36] (1903) 193 U. S. 197, 360–4.

words, the plain intent and purport of the Sherman Anti-Trust Act cannot be defeated by a resort to the sham and subterfuge of incorporation.

In *United States* v. *Milwaukee Refrigerator Transit Company*,[37] a dummy corporation was formed in order to evade the provisions of the Interstate Commerce Act and of the Elkins Act of 1903. The Pabst Brewing Company, which had organized the Transit Company in order thus indirectly to obtain illegal rebates, raised the usual stereotyped hue and cry of distinct corporate entity. Although the evidence showed that the Transit Company was merely the *alter ego* of the Brewing Company, that they were substantially identical in interest and control, that the dummy Transit Company could have been organized only with intent to evade the law, although the Brewing Company was the ultimate beneficiary, yet it was strenuously, nay vehemently, insisted "that a corporation is a legal entity" and that the government was remediless. The court exploded the theory of the defense, hoisted the distinguished counsel on their own petard and,—indicating that the Transit Company was a mere separate name for the Brewing Company, being in fact the same collection of persons and inter-

[37] (1905) 142 Fed. 247 (*per* Sanborn, J.).

65

ests,—stamped the device adopted as "neither new, nor deserving of any success." In other words, people cannot obtain legal immunity for deliberate wrongdoing by a resort to the "entity bath." Or, otherwise expressed, statutes cannot be violated by a resort to the corporate subterfuge. Courts will break away from the notion that a corporation is only a legal entity whenever its literal application would operate abortively.

The burning words of a late Chancellor of New Jersey should be borne in mind by every corporation lawyer who seeks to use the concept of corporate entity to defeat the end for which it was invented:[38]

"' * * * A more flimsy device, when the particulars are once known, it is impossible to imagine. It may succeed for a time in baffling persons. * * *'

"It must not be thought that courts are powerless to strip off disguises that are designed to thwart the purposes of the law. The mere suggestion of such a condition is an insult to the intelligence of the judiciary. Whenever such disguises are made apparent they can readily be disrobed. The difficulty is in showing the disguises, not in penetrating them when they appear."

A recent decision, following numerous others, by the United States Supreme Court, speaking through

[38] *Stockton* v. *Central R. R. Co.* (1892), 50 N. J. Eq. 52, 75–6, citing abundant authority.

the late Justice Harlan, emphasizes another phase of the disregard of corporate entity where the corporation is a mere shift to evade the law. In that case, a corporation was formed for the sole purpose of attempting to get a certain litigation into the federal courts and thus of invoking federal rather than state jurisdiction. The entity was impatiently, almost contemptuously, disregarded.[39]

Further illustrations *ad infinitum* might be given; they would serve not so much further to fortify this principle as to introduce needless repetition.

In cases involving an attempt to monopolize, it has of late become most necessary, both from a just and a practical standpoint, to look behind the corporate body and recognize the individual members. The leading case, and one of the most famous of these holdings, is *People* v. *North River Sugar Refining Company*.[40] Proceedings in *quo warranto* were brought against the company by the state of New York to deprive it of its corporate franchise for the reason that it had abused its rights and obligations by becoming a party to a forbidden and wholly illegal trust agreement. The corporation insisted

---

[39] *Miller and Lux* v. *East Side Canal, etc., Company* (1908), 211 U. S. 293, and cases cited.

[40] (1890) 121 N. Y. 582.

that it had never entered into the contract, but it appeared that the contract was signed by each and every shareholder. It was strenuously argued by as able counsel as were then at the New York bar, Messrs. James C. Carter and John E. Parsons, that the agreements were those only of the individual shareholders in their private capacities and with regard to their private property, and hence not corporate action or misconduct. It was contended that the absence of any formal action by the directors of the corporation proved that it, the entity, was free from guilt. It was urged that the illegal combination was the result merely of dealings and acts of the stockholders and not of any corporate action and that, therefore, the entity was not chargeable with any wrongdoing or misbehavior. The Court of Appeals affirmed the judgment of dissolution rendered in the court below and charged the entity with the acts of the stockholders and officers, deciding that under the circumstances of the case their acts were the acts of the corporation itself.

The court pointed out the utter ridiculousness of the appellant's argument that "while all that was human and could act had sinned, yet the impalpable entity had not acted at all and must go free."[41]

[41] (1890) 121 N. Y. at p. 619.

OF CORPORATE ENTITY

The stockholders, the acting and living men and women, had been guilty of misconduct. It would be nothing short of absurd to say that, although they were guilty, the corporate robe that enveloped them was spotless and they must, *a fortiori*, be left to wear it free and undisturbed. The scope of this article does not warrant a consideration of the monopolistic aspect of the decision. For present purposes, it is sufficient to note that the court ignored the corporate concept, brushed aside the entity and did not hesitate to "look beneath it at the actions of the individuals upon whom the franchise was conferred." As said by Judge Finch in his learned opinion:

" * * * The State gave the franchise, the charter, not to the impalpable, intangible and almost nebulous fiction of our thought, but to the corporators, the individuals, the acting and living men, to be used by them, to redound to their benefit, to strengthen their hand, and add energy to their capital. * * * The benefit is theirs, the punishment is theirs, and both must attend and depend upon their conduct; and when they all act, collectively, as an aggregate body, without the least exception, and so acting, reach results and accomplish purposes clearly corporate in their character, and affecting the vitality, the independence, the utility, of the corporation ·itself, we cannot hesitate to conclude that there has been corporate conduct which the state may review, and not be defeated by the assumed innocence of a convenient fiction. * * * '' [42]

The justice of this decision is clear. To hold otherwise would be to ignore the real and substantial parties in interest, blinding the eyes not only to the facts but to the justice of the situation, and, admitting the sins of the body, to insist that the sinner remains pure.

Two years after the decision of the New York court, a similar decision was rendered by the Supreme Court of Ohio, in the now famous case of *State* v. *Standard Oil Company*.[43] In that case all, or at least a great majority, of the stockholders comprising a corporation, entered into an illegal trust agreement in their individual capacities for the purpose of concealing the real nature and object of their actions. The property and business of the company were affected in the same manner and to the same extent as if there had been a formal resolution of the Board of Directors. To prevent the abuse of corporate power, the state of Ohio challenged the proceedings by an action of *quo warranto*. The able attorneys for the Standard Oil Company, Joseph H. Choate and S. C. T. Dodd

---

[42] (1890) 121 N. Y. at p. 622.   [43] (1892) 49 Oh. St. 137.

among them, again raised the plea of corporate
entity. They urged in the first point of their brief
that:

"It is a modern heresy, largely invented during the
late crusade against the principle of association in
business, that a corporation is not a 'legal entity,'
but simply an association of stockholders with certain
legal faculties. * * * " [44]

They claimed that the legal entity could not be
affected by any acts or agreements except such as
were executed in formal manner on its behalf by
its corporate agencies. The Supreme Court of Ohio
reached the same result as the New York Court of
Appeals, strangely enough not citing or quoting
from the *North River Sugar Refining Co.* decision.
The Attorney General, however, had called the
court's attention to that case.[45]

An extract from the learned opinion of Minshall,
J., indicates the court's attitude:

" * * * Disregarding the mere fiction of a separate
legal entity, since to regard it in an inquiry like the one
before us would be subversive of the purpose for which
it was invented, is there, upon an analysis of the agreement, room for doubt, that the act of all the stockholders, officers and directors of the company in signing it,
should be imputed to them as an act done in their

[44] (1892) 49 Oh. St. at p. 167.   [45] *Ibid.* 163.

PIERCING THE VEIL

capacity as a corporation? We think not, since thereby all the property and business of the company is, and was intended to be, virtually transferred to the Standard Oil Trust, and is controlled, through its trustees, as effectually as if a formal transfer had been made by the directors of the company. * * * " [46]

The decision is notable as marking again the intention of a court of last resort to ignore the concept of corporate entity whenever and wherever extended to an intent and purpose unreasonably and illegally to restrain trade, or to monopolize or to seek to monopolize, and, therefore, not within the reason or policy of the concept. To permit the notion of legal entity to stand in the way of a decision which justice and public policy requires, to allow a metaphysical theory and concept to interfere with state control of corporations, to permit restraint of trade and monopoly itself to be achieved under the guise of refined and abstruse theoretical reasoning, or lack of reasoning,—is abhorrent to the genius and spirit of both the common law and chancery. To the credit of our courts, it must be conceded that when tried in the balance they have not been found wanting, in this important regard.

Still one other line of decisions admirably illus-

OF CORPORATE ENTITY

trates the refusal to permit monopoly to be attained under the cover of corporate entity. As good examples as any, of this second phase, are the decisions of the Supreme Court of Illinois in the Milk and Whiskey Trust cases. In the former case,[47] the astute counsel for the monopoly urged, apparently in all seriousness, that the Milk Shippers Association, which had been incorporated, could not be guilty of illegal combination, because the corporation, as an entity, could not enter into a trust or combination with itself. The court's unhesitating answer to this climax of "entity" sophistry was that the actions of the individual shareholders could be regarded, and, if they had, together with the entity, combined, they were all alike guilty. In other words, incorporation will not render a combination legal on the ground that the corporation cannot alone enter into a trust, as the *acts of the corporation are those of the associated persons as individuals*. Mr. Justice Phillips, speaking for the court, said:

" * * * There can be no immunity for evasion of the policy of the State by its own creations. The corporation, as an entity, may not be able to create a

[47] *Ford* v. *Chicago Milk Shippers Association* (1895), 155 Ill. 166.

trust or combination with itself, but its individual shareholders may, in controlling it, together with it, create such trust or combination that will constitute it, with them, alike guilty." [48]

In the same year, the same court decided that the attempt of the whiskey trust [49] to purge itself of illegality by changing its form of organization from an unincorporated association, or "trust," to a corporation was ineffectual. The court drew aside the veil of entity and rightly said that if the trust agreement was repugnant to public policy and illegal, "it is impossible to see why the same is not true of the corporation which succeeds to it and takes its place."

In the light of these decisions, it is clear that there is no magic in incorporation which can purge a monopolizing scheme of its slimy, greedy viciousness. If illegal before incorporation, it is equally illegal afterwards, and for the same reasons. The legal armor-plate can be torn aside and the acts of the flesh and blood associates disclosed and scrutinized. [50]

[48] *Ibid.* 180.

[49] *Distilling and Cattle Feeding Co.* v. *People* (1895), 156 Ill. 448, 490–2.

[50] See, also, *Anthony* v. *American Glucose Co.* (1895), 146 N. Y. 407; *Harding* v. *American Glucose Co.* (1899), 182 Ill.

OF CORPORATE ENTITY

The freely transferable nature of shares of corporate stock oftentimes necessitates a disregard of the entity concept. For example, X has an equitable claim against the Y corporation, because of a corporate fraud upon X in the inducement of a contract. Unquestionably X is entitled to a rescission of the transaction. However, if X delays the assertion of his rights for a long period and meanwhile innocent purchasers have acquired an interest in the corporate property, as shareholders or creditors, a court of chancery would be warranted oftentimes in drawing aside the web of entity and taking cognizance of the human factors.[51]

Again, where the body of stockholders is so circumstanced that no relief should be afforded them, may the corporate entity recover? Will the court adhere to the doctrine at the expense of justice and common sense, or will the stumbling block be pushed aside? The ablest decision in point known to the writer is that of Dean Roscoe

551, 615 *et seq.; Dunbar* v. *American Telephone & Telegraph Co.* (1906), 224 Ill. 9, 25. But see *Edmunds* v. *I. C. R. R. Co.* (Ill. 1908), 36 Nat. Corp. Rep. 50, and comment thereon in 8 Columbia Law Review 320.

[51] *Cf. U. S.* v. *San Jacinto Tin Co.* (1885), 23 Fed. 279; *Wetmore* v. *St. Paul R. R. Co.* (1880), 3 Fed. 177; 1 Morawetz, Private Corporations, § 231.

75

PIERCING THE VEIL

Pound, when a Commissioner of the Supreme Court of Nebraska, the precise situation being presented for his consideration in *Home Fire Insurance Company* v. *Barber*.[52] Declaring that it would be a reproach upon the courts if they could not look behind the corporation to the ultimate beneficiaries, the court denied relief to the corporation. If the stockholders have no standing, and if they are not equitably entitled to the relief sought to be enforced by the corporation in their behalf, the corporation itself will not be permitted to recover. As said by Pound, C:

"* * * When the corporation comes into equity and seeks equitable relief, we ought to look at the substance of the proceeding, and if the beneficiaries of the judgment sought have no standing in equity to recover, we ought not to become befogged by the fiction of corporate individuality, and apply the principles of equity to reach an inequitable result." [53]

The case commented upon arose in equity but the rule is by no means peculiar to that jurisdiction. Oftentimes in courts of law, as has already been seen, analogous reasoning has been applied.[54]

[52] (1903) 67 Neb. 644.

[53] *Ibid.* 669.

[54] See, also, *Ark. River, etc., Co.* v. *Farmers' Loan & Trust Co.* (1889), 13 Colo. 587, *Chicago Union Traction Co.* v. *City*

OF CORPORATE ENTITY

Closely allied to the foregoing lines of decisions is
the disregard of the entity theory where acts have
been undertaken by the entire body of stockholders
and attempt then made to escape liability "by
conjuring with the corporate name." These cases do
not, as in the *Sugar Refining and Standard Oil* decisions, involve any attempt to monopolize, but their
reasoning and argumentation are, naturally, quite
similar. The courts perforce are obliged to consider
that the individual members are, in the last analysis,
the true parties in interest.[55]

Few judges have ever been sufficiently foolhardy
to seek to sit in cases where a party plaintiff or
defendant was a corporation in which the judge held
shares of stock. In an early New York case,[56] a
judge regarded himself as competent to sit under
such circumstances, relying upon the distinction between the corporation and its shareholders. It is
true, forsooth, that the shareholders do not appear
upon the formal record, yet are they not the parties

of Chicago (1902), 199 Ill. 579; *Des Moines Gas Co.* v. *West*
(1878), 50 Iowa 16.

[55] *Sheldon Hat Blocking Co.* v. *Eickemeyer Hat Blocking
Machine Co.* (1882), 90 N. Y. 607, 613; *Hotel Co.* v. *Wade*
(1877), 97 U. S. 13, 23.

[56] *Stuart* v. *Mechanics' & Farmers' Bank* (N. Y., 1822),
19 Johns. 496, 501.

77

in substance and the corporation but the party in form? In the next year, Chancellor Sanford had the same question before him. The Washington Insurance Company, in which he was a stockholder, instituted suit in his tribunal. The learned judge immediately directed that all proceedings before him cease and refused to take jurisdiction on the ground that the stockholders were "the real litigants in the suit." [57] The view of Chancellor Sanford is that universally adopted by courts to-day. In all such cases, so far as the writer knows, the veil of corporate entity is lifted aside.[58]

The entity theory, it stands to reason, often must be ignored in stockholders' suits for mismanagement, in determining the rights of the stockholders *inter sese* in equity in cases of ratification, and in working out problems bearing upon the consolidation and dissolution of corporations. In these cases, however, the disregard of the concept of corporate entity is incidental rather than fundamental.

A few courts have argued that a corporation

[57] *Washington Ins. Co.* v. *Price* (N. Y., 1825), 1 Hopkins Ch. 1.

[58] *State* v. *Young* (1893), 31 Fla. 594; *Inhabitants of Northampton* v. *Smith* (Mass., 1846), 11 Metc. 390; *Gregory* v. *Cleveland R. R. Co.* (1855), 4 Oh. St. 675; *Newcome* v. *Light* (1882), 58 Tex. 141 (*Semble*).

should not be recognized as a separate entity when its stock is owned wholly by one person.[59] It has been insisted, especially in the Supreme Court of Maryland, that when one person owns all the shares of stock of a corporation, he, by virtue of such ownership, becomes the owner of the corporate property, may sell and dispose of it, if he chooses to do so, and, in short, becomes the corporation. This, however, is a minority view and has met with little favor. It is true that courts will be more apt to pierce the veil of corporate entity where one person owns all the corporate stock, but they do this in such cases not because it is a one-man company, not because there is but one shareholder, but because the other circumstances of the case make such action imperative. The writer submits that in practically every case of a one-man corporation where the veil of entity was brushed aside, the same result would have followed had there been a thousand stockholders, or ten thousand. Outside of Maryland, fortunately, there are but few heterodox decisions. One of the most notorious is a comparatively recent holding of the Supreme Court of Alabama. In *First National Bank of Gadsen* v.

[59] *Swift* v. *Smith, Dixon & Co.* (1886), 65 Md. 428, 434; *The Bellona Company's Case* (Md. 1831), 3 Bland, 442 (*Semble*).

Winchester,[60] it was held that a mortgage of corporate property by the only two stockholders of the company was valid although no corporate action had been taken. The decision relied upon the reasoning of the Maryland courts.

The cases which hold that the only stockholder in the corporation, or the only two or three stockholders in a corporation, become the corporation itself and can deal with the corporate property *ad libitum* are marked, it is true, by a disregard of the theory of corporate entity, but the disregard is an unsound and erroneous one. It is just in this class of case, standing on such facts *per se*, that the doctrine of corporate entity should be adhered to. The writer does not mean to intimate that, if in these cases any of the elements previously mentioned which warrant a disregard of the doctrine of corporate entity are present, the concept should nevertheless be adhered to. What is meant is this: that simply because a company is reduced in number to one or two, or a very few, stockholders, does not warrant for a single instant, *per se*, the disregard of the corporate entity. Whether there is one shareholder in a corporation or whether there are ten thousand makes no difference, in other words, un-

[60] (1898) 119 Ala. 168.

OF CORPORATE ENTITY

less some of the circumstances aforementioned which warrant a disregard of the theory of corporate entity are present.

A moment's thought and consideration will make clear the reason. Stockholders, as such have no title to corporate property.[61] Stockholders are not tenants in common of the corporate property.[62] In order to keep the title to corporate property free from complication and uncertainty, it has been found absolutely essential for the administration of justice to treat a corporation as a collective entity without regard to its individual shareholders.[63] One illustration will suffice. Suppose X and Y became the sole stockholders in a corporation. If they were permitted to sell, mortgage or otherwise dispose of the corporate property by virtue thereof, titles could not be kept clear, and chaos, confusion and hopeless uncertainty would result.[64] The writer, although a firm believer in the necessity for a frequent and liberal disregard of the concept of corporate entity, believes that to ignore it simply

[61] Pound, C., in *Home Fire Insurance Co.* v. *Barber* (1903), 67 Neb. 644, 668.

[62] *Harton* v. *Johnston* (1910), 166 Ala. 317, 322.

[63] *Gallagher* v. *Germania Brewing Co.* (1893), 53 Minn. 214.

[64] Remarks of Mitchell, J., in *Gallagher* v. *Germania Brewing Co.*, *supra*.

because the number of stockholders has become very few, or even one, is to convert an otherwise sane, safe and sensible policy into a *reductio ad absurdum;* and so, to their credit, the majority of American courts have universally held. [65]

The correct doctrine to adopt in these cases, as opposed to that of the wayward Maryland and Alabama courts, is well illustrated in a leading Minnesota decision.[66]   In that case, one King, the owner of all the stock in a corporation, executed a deed in his own name of certain realty owned by

[65] *Spencer* v. *Champion* (1833), 9 Conn. 535; *Exchange Bank* v. *Macon Construction Co.* (1895), 97 Ga. 1; *Sellers* v. *Greer* (1898), 172 Ill. 549; *Coal Belt Co.* v. *Peabody Coal Co.* (1907), 230 Ill. 164, 168; *Hopkins* v. *Roseclaire Lead Co.* (1874), 72 Ill. 373, 379; *Allemong* v. *Simmons* (1890), 124 Ind. 199; *George T. Stagg Co.* v. *Taylor* (1902), 113 Ky. 709, 718; *In Matter of Belton* (1895), 47 La. An. 1614; *Ulmer* v. *Lime Rock R. R. Co.* (1904), 98 Me. 579, 594; *Old Dominion Copper Co.* v. *Bigelow* (1909), 203 Mass. 159, 192; *Rough* v. *Breitung* (1898), 117 Mich. 48; *Baldwin* v. *Canfield* (1879), 26 Minn. 43; *Palmer* v. *Ring* (N. Y., 1906), 113 App. Div. 643, 99 N. Y. Supp. 290 and cases therein cited; *Central Mfg. Co.* v. *Montgomery* (1910), 144 Mo. App. 494; *Commonwealth* v. *Monongahela Bridge Co.* (1906), 216 Pa. St. 108; *Rhawn* v. *Edge Hill Furnace Co.* (1902), 201 Pa. St. 637; *Kendall* v. *Klappherthal Co.* (1902), 202 Pa. St. 596; *Parker* v. *Bethel Hotel Co.* (1896), 96 Tenn. 252; *Button* v. *Hoffman* (1884), 61 Wis. 20. But see *Buffalo Loan Co.* v. *Medina Gas Co.* (1896), 42 N. Y. Supp. 781, 788; affirmed, 162 N. Y. 67.

[66] *Baldwin* v. *Canfield, supra.*

it. Subsequently thereto an equitable action was brought by a stockholder to have the deed declared void as a cloud on the title of the corporation. It was unanimously held that the deed was "void upon its face" and therefore not a cloud upon title, "being the deed of a total stranger to the title." A famous Wisconsin decision, in which it was held that a sole stockholder could not maintain an action of replevin for corporate property illegally taken by the defendant, illustrates, in another manner, the correct holding.[67]

To reduce this proposition to the form of a rule: corporate entity will not be ignored at law or equity simply because the number of stockholders is few, or even one, unless the circumstances are such as would warrant the same disregard of the entity were there ten thousand shareholders. As a corollary to this, it follows, in the absence of such extraneous circumstances, that, where a question of title to corporate property is involved, the concept must faithfully be adhered to, though there be but one stockholder, under the penalty of an otherwise inextricable confusion.

The various classes of cases where the concept of corporate entity should be ignored and the veil

[67] *Button* v. *Hoffman, supra.*

83

drawn aside have now been briefly reviewed. What general rule, if any, can be laid down? The nearest approximation to generalization which the present state of the authorities would warrant is this: When the conception of corporate entity is employed to defraud creditors, to evade an existing obligation, to circumvent a statute, to achieve or perpetuate monopoly, or to protect knavery or crime, the courts will draw aside the web of entity, will regard the corporate company as an association of live, up-and-doing, men and women shareholders, and will do justice between real persons. This is particularly true in courts of equity, but finds many illustrations in courts of law as well, for it must not be thought that "Our Lady of the Common Law" is not sufficiently powerful to explode sophistry or scholastic theory where used as a cloak for wrongdoing. In neither tribunal is the concept exalted into a fetish to be worshiped "in the sacrifice of those who, in the last analysis, are the real parties in interest." [68]

The successive decisions of the courts indicate a willingness to adjust the entity theory to the ever-growing complexities and constantly increasing problems of the modern private corporation. Again

[68] Lamar, J., in *Oliver* v. *Oliver* (1903), 118 Ga. 362; *cf. Percival* v. *Wright*, L. R. (1902), 2 Ch. 421.

and again, the entity doctrine, and even the rule
of *stare decisis*, have not been permitted to stand
in the way of the achievement of substantial rug-
ged justice. There could be no better refutation
of the charge so frequently made *horis novissimis*
that courts are inelastic, unyielding and unwilling
to respond to social and economic facts than the
adjustment—still in process—of corporate concepts
to modern business facts. Of course, it stands to
reason that the courts lag somewhat behind corporate business; forsooth, cases do not arise until
transactions have been engaged in and brought
before the courts for a decision. In the main,
however, and on the whole, the response has been
prompt, certain, and sufficient.[69]

[69] This paper has been cited frequently by the courts and
law writers; see *Ross* v. *Jacobowitz*, 216 App. Div. 184, 187,
214 N. Y. Supp. 514, 517; *Farmers' Loan & Trust Co.* v.
Pierson, 130 Misc. Rep. 110, 222 N. Y. Supp. 532, 541; 36
Yale Law Journal, 254–260; 14 Calif. Law Review, 12; 100
Central Law Journal, 107, 111; Fletcher, Cyclopedia of Law
of Corporations, Vol. 1, 49, 61; Clark, Corporations (3d ed.),
p. 13.

Voting Rights and the Doctrine of Corporate Entity [1]

CORPORATION A owns all the stock of corporation B. The latter is run as a subsidiary of the former. The officers of each are substantially identical. They have separate boards of directors with varying members and they maintain distinct sets of books. Their existence as separate organizations is preserved. Corporation B owns, let us say, one hundred shares of stock in corporation A. The question is, can it lawfully vote them? Could the stock held by the subsidiary corporation in the corporation controlling it, be voted upon the issue of the dissolution of the latter, for example?

The decisions at common law were in conflict as to whether a corporation had implied power to hold stock in another corporation. The English cases hold "that there is not, either by the common or statute law, anything to prohibit one trading corporation from taking or accepting shares in another trading corporation."[2] The Ohio cases, followed in

[1] Fordham Law Review, Vol. 2 (1916).

[2] *In re Asiatic Banking Corporation*, L. R., 4 Ch. App. Cas. 252; *Booth* v. *Robinson*, 55 Md. 419, *Accord*.

many American jurisdictions, hold, on the other
hand, "that one corporation cannot become the
owner of any portion of the capital stock of another
corporation, unless authority to become such is
clearly conferred by statute." [3]   And, says the
Ohio court, "were this not so, one corporation, by
buying up the majority of the shares of the stock of
another, could take the entire management of its
business, however foreign such business might be to
that which the corporation so purchasing said
shares was created to carry on. A banking corporation could become the operator of a railroad, or
carry on the business of manufacturing, and any
other corporation could engage in banking by obtaining the control of the bank's stock." [4] It might
be urged that such an acquisition, as the Ohio court
mentions, is *ultra vires*, not because the purchase is
stock, but because the business is outside the scope
of the charter of the purchasing corporation.[5] In

[3] *Franklin Bank* v. *Commercial Bank*, 36 Oh. St. 350; *Byrne*
v. *Schuyler Mfg. Co.*, 65 Conn. 336, 31 Atl. 833; *People* v. *Chicago Gas Trust Co.*, 130 Ill. 268, 22 N. E. 798; *Woodberry* v.
McClurg, 78 Miss. 831, 29 So. 514; *Holmes Mfg. Co.* v. *Holmes
Metal Co.*, 127 N. Y. 252, 27 N. E. 831; *Easun* v. *Buckeye Brewing Co.*, 51 Fed. 156, *Accord*.

[4] *Franklin Bank* v. *Commercial Bank*, *supra*.

[5] See *Hill* v. *Nisbet*, 100 Ind. 341. The correct test is, at
common law, whether the purchase is reasonably incidental to,

New York, the difficult question, and its corollary—the validity of the holding company—were put to rest by statutory enactment, which not only gives to one corporation the right to hold stock in another, but further contemplates, at least inferentially, the ownership by one corporation of the entire capital stock of another.[6]

We start, therefore, with the hypothesis that there is nothing in the written law of this state which forbids one corporation from holding even the entire capital stock of another corporation, or causes thereby the destruction of their separate corporate existence. If corporation B is a distinct legal entity from corporation A, why cannot it hold stock in an-

and consequential upon, the authorized corporate objects. This depends on the surrounding circumstances.

[6] Sec. 52. Purchase of Stock of Other Corporations. Any stock corporation, domestic or foreign, now existing or hereafter organized, except moneyed corporations, may purchase, acquire, hold and dispose of the stocks, bonds and other evidences of indebtedness of any corporation, domestic or foreign, and issue in exchange therefor its stock, bonds or other obligations if authorized so to do by a provision in the certificate of incorporation of such stock corporation, or in any certificate amendatory thereof or supplementary thereto, filed in pursuance of law, or if the corporation whose stock is so purchased, acquired, held or disposed of, is engaged in a business similar to that of such stock corporation, or engaged in the manufacture, use or sale of the property, or in the construction or operation of works necessary or useful in the business of such

other corporation, namely, corporation A, and possess, as incident to its ownership of the stock, the voting rights appurtenant thereto? But, on the other hand, it may be asked, how can corporation B fairly be permitted to vote its shares in corporation A, since to permit this would be tantamount to allowing corporation A to vote shares of itself owned by itself? These questions strike so deeply into the roots of corporation law that their evasion can hardly be thought of.

At the outset, let it stand admitted that a corporation cannot vote its own stock. The cases so hold, and their doctrine is in accord with the dictates of sound public policy.[7] In fact, it is elementary that "a corporation may not vote shares of its own

stock corporation, or in which or in connection with which the manufactured articles, product or property of such stock corporation are or may be used, or is a corporation with which such stock corporation is or may be authorized to consolidate. When any such corporation shall be a stockholder in any other corporation, as herein provided, its president or other officers shall be eligible to the office of director of such corporation, the same as if they were individually stockholders therein and the corporation holding such stock shall possess and exercise in respect thereof, all the rights, powers and privileges of individual owners or holders of such stock. (Stock Corp. Law, N. Y.) [This section is now N. Y. Stock Corp. Law, § 18, with minor changes of wording.]

[7] *Ex parte Holmes*, 5 Cow. (N. Y.), 426; Cook, Corps. (7th ed.), § 613.

stock held by it, either directly or indirectly by a trustee." [8]

Conceding this, it is erroneous to affirm that it follows that corporation B cannot vote the shares of stock which it owns in corporation A. That begs the question. It assumes that corporation B and corporation A are but one entity in the eye of the law, and that, therefore, corporation A is voting shares of its own stock. Mere identity of stock ownership does not make two corporations one and the same. This last proposition, however, is by no means universally conceded. It has become increasingly the fashion of late to urge that, even when the same group of associates, acting with a common purpose, assumes two really separate corporate organizations, the separate entity of the two organizations is a mere sham, an empty mask, and that the law may and will strip away the mask and look to the actual persons behind it. [9] The contention is—how can a mere process of duplicate corporate christening create distinct juridical personalities, how can the law treat

[8] See paper, "The Power of a Corporation to Acquire Its Own Stock," 24 Yale Law Journal, 177, 184, collecting the authorities.

[9] This was one of the Government's chief contentions in the case of *United States* v. *Delaware, Lackawanna & Western R. Co.*, 238 U. S. 516, reversing 213 Fed. 240.

DOCTRINE OF CORPORATE ENTITY

these corporate Dromios [10] as other than one and
the same? However plausible this argument may
appear, it cannot be upheld by the courts in cases
where the two corporations are really separate and
distinct, without striking at the bed-rock principle
of corporateness, namely, the existence of the corporation as a juristic person separate and distinct
from its members. [11] A corporation is much like an
expansible symbol, for instance, a bracket in an algebraic expression; which, while treated as a unit, is
nevertheless capable at any time of being expanded
to show its real constituency. It is logically manda-
tory that the distinction between the corporation, as
a legal unit, and its members, be maintained. Would
even the most radical contend that the United States
Steel Corporation and the Southern Pacific Railroad
Company are one and the same, because, by some
chance, their stockholders on a given date are identical? The proposition that two corporations are
identical merely because their stock ownership is the
same or substantially the same, is not merely un-

[10] Shakespeare's Comedy of Errors, Act V, Scene 1.

[11] *People's Pleasure Park Co.* v. *Rohleder*, 109 Va. 439, 61
S. E. 794, 63 S. E. 981, holding a corporation is not a "colored
person," though it is admittedly "composed exclusively of ne-
groes." The Civil Law rule is the same. La. Civ. Code,
Arts. 427, 432, 435, 436. And see *Mioton* v. *Del Corral*, 132
La. 730, 61 So. 771.

orthodox—it is revolutionary. It ignores the basic conception of corporation law.

The leading case in this country is *Button* v. *Hoffman*.[12] It was there held that the owner of all the capital stock of a corporation could not bring a replevin suit in his own name to recover certain corporate personalty, since he is not the corporation, and since "while the corporation exists he is a mere stockholder of it and nothing else." And it is also the rule that the circumstance that the owner of all the stock is another corporation "makes no difference in principle."[13] To the same effect are numerous authorities.[14] This doctrine, that the most distinctive attribute of the corporate type of business organization is its existence as a legal entity

[12] 61 Wis. 20, 20 N. W. 667, cited with approval in *State* v. *Tacoma Ry. & Power Co.*, 61 Wash. 507, 112 Pac. 506.

[13] *Exchange Bank of Macon* v. *Macon Const. Co.*, 97 Ga. 1, 25 S. E. 326.

[14] *Spencer* v. *Champion*, 9 Conn. 535; *Newton Mfg. Co.* v. *White*, 42 Ga. 148; *Hopkins* v. *Roseclare Lead Co.*, 72 Ill. 373; *Allemong* v. *Simmons*, 124 Ind. 199; *Stagg Co.* v. *Taylor*, 113 Ky. 709; *In the Matter of Belton*, 47 La. Ann. 1614; *England* v. *Dearborn*, 141 Mass. 590; *Ulmer* v. *Lime Rock R. Co.*, 98 Me. 579; *Rough* v. *Breitung*, 117 Mich. 48; *Baldwin* v. *Canfield*, 26 Minn. 43; *Central Mfg. Co.* v. *Montgomery*, 144 Mo. App. 494; *Monongahela Bridge Co.* v. *Pittsburg Tract. Co.*, 196 Pa. St. 25; *Rhawn* v. *Furnace Co.*, 201 Pa. St. 637; *Parker* v. *Bethel Hotel Co.*, 96 Tenn. 252; *Aiello* v. *Crampton*, 201 Fed. 891; 120 C. C. A. 189. But see *Swift* v. *Smith*, 65 Md. 428.

distinct and apart from the stockholders, is a necessary one. Any other rule "would result in the
worst sort of complication,"[15] particularly where
titles to property might be involved. The New York
decisions are in accord, and adhere to the entity doctrine,[16] unless fraud or its equivalent be proven dis-
tinctly.[17] In a notable case,[18] Miller, J., said:

> "It is well settled that the title to corporate
> property is in the corporate entity and not in
> its stockholders (*Saranac & L. P. R. R. Co.* v.
> *Arnold*, 167 N. Y. 368; *Buffalo L. T. & S. D. Co.* v.
> *Medina Gas Co.*, 162 N. Y. 67), and, as the trans-
> fer made by Schwickart did not purport to be
> a corporate act, it was manifestly insufficient to
> transfer the corporate property, although he
> may have owned substantially all of the stock."

The English cases take the same point of view.
Where all the shares of a German company were

[15] *Gallagher* v. *Germania Brewing Co.*, 53 Minn. 214, 54 N.
W. 1115.

[16] *Stone* v. *Cleveland &c. R. Co.*, 202 N. Y. 352; *Saranac R.
Co.* v. *Arnold*, 167 N. Y. 368; *Buffalo Loan Co.* v. *Medina Gas
Co.*, 162 N. Y. 67; *Irvine* v. *N. Y. Edison Co.*, 207 N. Y. 425;
Palmer v. *Ring*, 113 App. Div. 643; *New York Air Brake Co.*
v. *International Steam Pump Co.*, 64 Misc. Rep. 347.

[17] *Goss & Co.* v. *Goss*, No. 2, 147 App. Div. 698; *Garrigues*
v. *International Agricult. Corp.*, 159 App. Div. 877, 880, *per*
Dowling, J.

[18] *Palmer* v. *Ring*, 113 App. Div. 643; 99 N. Y. Supp.
290.

owned by an English company, the court held that this fact "does not make the German company a mere alias, or a trustee, or an agent for the English company, or for the stockholders in the English company," [19] and declared that: "The German company is an existing person and a different entity from the English company."

During the late European conflict, the English courts made several interesting applications of the doctrine of corporate entity. Of 25,000 shares of stock of a company incorporated in England, all the shares except 2 shares were held by alien enemies, to wit, Germans. The corporation brought suit against a certain other corporation in an English court. It was held entitled to sue.[20] The decision is sound. The alien enemy character of the shareholders did not alter the English

[19] *Gramophone & Typewriter, Ltd.*, v. *Stanley*, L. R. (1906), 2 K. B. 856, (1908), 2 K. B. 89. The decision is rested on the decision of the House of Lords in *Salomon* v. *Salomon & Co.*, L. R. (1897), App. Cas. 22. The Supreme Judicial Court of Massachusetts recently rendered a much similar decision. *Brighton Packing Co.* v. *Butchers' Slaughtering & Melting Ass'n*, 211 Mass. 398; *Contra, Andres* v. *Morgan*, 62 Oh. St. 236.

[20] *Continental Tyre & Rubber Co., Ltd.*, v. *Daimler Co., Ltd.*, 138 L. T. J. (C. A.), 272; (1915), 1 K. B. 893; 138 L. T. J., 83. [Reversed on other grounds (1916), 2 A. C. 307; see 17 Col. L. R. 132; 30 Harv. L. R. 83.]

DOCTRINE OF CORPORATE ENTITY

domicile and citizenship of the corporation.[21] The decision resembles the well-known early case of *Queen* v. *Arnaud*.[22] An English statute forbade the registration of any vessel owned by foreigners, "in whole or in part, directly or indirectly." A corporation chartered by England, whose chief stockholders were foreigners, sought to compel the registry of its vessel. It was held that the vessel should be registered. This may strike some persons as anomalous also, but it is quite correct.[23]

From the foregoing discussion, it follows that Corporation A and Corporation B should be regarded by the courts as two separate legal persons. They are not the same juridical entity in any sense of the word. The general rule is that the holder of the legal title to shares of stock is entitled to vote them. When the laws of the state in which a corporation is organized authorize the holding of

[21] Of course, none of the proceeds of the suit, in the event of success could be remitted to the enemy shareholders, thus avoiding giving aid to an alien enemy.

[22] 9 Q. B. (Adol. & El.) 806.

[23] See, also, *Humphreys* v. *McKissock*, 140 U. S. 304; *In re Watertown Paper Co.*, 169 Fed. 252, 94 C. C. A. 528, *per* Noyes, J. In *McCaskill Co.* v. *United States*, Mr. Justice McKenna recently said: "Undoubtedly a corporation is in law, a person or entity entirely distinct from its stockholders and officers." (216 U. S. 504, 514.)

its stock by other corporations, another corporation holding stock therein and having authority
to do so, may vote the stock to the same extent
as any other stockholder.[24]   This is fortified in
New York by the statutory provision which confers upon corporate stockholders "all the rights,
powers and privileges" of individual stockholders
thus conferring the right to vote, if not expressly,
at least by reasonable implication.[25]   And, it has
been held in this state that a corporation holding
stock in another corporation possesses all the
rights of a natural holder, including the right to
vote.[26]   Hence, Corporation B, as the owner of
one hundred shares of Corporation A, should be
entitled to vote them.   Despite the ownership by
Corporation A of all the stock of Corporation B,
this is, in no respect, a voting by Corporation A of
shares of its own stock.[27]

[24] *Rogers* v. *Nashville R. Co.*, 91 Fed. 299, 33 C. C. A. 517;
Davis v. *U. S. Elec. Co.*, 77 Md. 35; *Oelberman* v. *N. Y. R. Co.*,
76 Hun, 613, 77 Hun, 332, 29 N. Y. Supp. 545.

[25] N. Y. Stock Corp. Law, § 52 [now § 18].   See ante, note 6.

[26] *In re Buffalo, etc., R. Co.*, 37 N. Y. Supp. 1048.

[27] See the decision of Ex-Judge Noyes, as referee, in *Lazenby*
v. *Int. Cotton Mills Corp., et al.*, modified 174 App. Div. 906,
160 N. Y. Supp. 1.   But see Vice Chancellor Pitney's decision in *O'Connor* v. *Int. Silver Co.*, 68 N. J. Eq. 67; affirmed
on quite distinct grounds on appeal (68 N. J. Eq. 680).

DOCTRINE OF CORPORATE ENTITY

The conclusion is, then, that Corporation B may lawfully vote the one hundred shares of stock which it owns in Corporation A. The corporations are distinct and separate legal entities. The fact that the shares of Corporation B all belong to Corporation A does not make Corporation B— to paraphrase the learned English judge—"a mere alias, or a trustee, or an agent for Corporation A, or for the shareholders in Corporation A." Since Corporation B, a distinct juristic person, has lawful title to one hundred shares of stock in Corporation A, and since voting rights follow legal title, statutory prohibitions apart, it follows that Corporation B is well within its rights in voting the shares which it holds of Corporation A. There is nothing anomalous in this result.

It should be noted that there is no suggestion in our hypothetical case of fraud or of disregard of the public interests. It is to ignore the entire theory of separate corporate existence to declare that one corporation is identical, in the eye of the law, with another in which it holds a controlling stock interest. But this doctrine of separate existence may be carried too far, and it is properly disregarded in cases of fraud, statutory circumvention, public wrong, and like instances.[28] "If any general rule can be laid down, in the present state of authority, it is that a corporation will be looked upon as a legal entity as a general rule, and until sufficient reason to the contrary appears; but, when the notion of legal entity is used to defeat public convenience, justify wrong, protect fraud, or defend crime, the law will regard the corporation as an association of persons." [29] In a noted English case, a German vessel owned by a German corporation, while sailing from Hamburg to London, was sold by telegraph on August 1, to an English corporation, controlled by the German corporation. On August 4, war was declared between Germany and England. Next day, the vessel arrived in England and was seized as a prize. The English corporation claimed that the

[28] See paper, "Piercing the Veil of Corporate Entity," 12 Columbia Law Review, 496.

[29] *United States* v. *Milwaukee Refrigerator Transit Co.*, 142 Fed. 247, 255, *per* Sanborn, J. The Appellate Division, First Dept., speaking through Dowling, J., said: "That the doctrine of corporate entity will not be allowed to stand in the way of circumventing fraud or administering justice, has been held in *Goss & Co.* v. *Goss*, *No. 2* (147 App. Div. 698)." *Garrigues* v. *International Agricult. Corporation*, 159 App. Div. 877, 880. The Supreme Court of the United States takes the same position. *Linn & Lane Timber Co.* v. *United States*, 236 U. S. 574.

transfer to it made the seizure illegal. The Prize
Court held the seizure proper and that the claim
was invalid.[30] The decision is sound. The transfer was not valid as it was made in contemplation
of war and to avoid seizure as a prize.[31] Under
such circumstances, the application of the doctrine
of distinct corporate entity, is uncalled for. Lord
Mansfield's classic rule as to the use of fictions of
law is applicable:

> "It is a certain rule that a fiction of law shall
> never be contradicted, so as to defeat the end
> for which it was invented, but for every other
> purpose it may be contradicted." (*Mostyn
> v. Fabriges*, Cowper, 177.)
>
> "Fictions of law hold only in respect of the
> rules and purposes for which they were invented;
> when they are urged to an intent and purpose
> not within the reason and policy of the fiction
> the other party may show the truth." (*Morris
> v. Pugh*, 3 Burr, 1243.)

It is often extremely difficult to draw the line.[32]
In determining when to refuse to apply the doctrine, however, it is serviceable to bear in mind
that "the purpose in making all corporations is

[30] *The Tommi*, 59 Sol. J. 26.
[31] See *The Ann Green*, 1 Gall. (U. S.) 274.
[32] See *Lavery* v. *Purssell* (1888), 39 Ch. Div. 508.

the accomplishment of some public good," [33] and that no rule of law or logic requires courts to employ the conception of separate corporate existence as a whitewash for corporate wrongdoing. The power of courts to frustrate wrongful devices is more than coextensive with the perverted ingenuity which devises them.

It follows that if Corporation B were organized, or the stock transfer made, in our hypothetical case, solely in order to achieve certain vicious and fraudulent results, the corporate fiction properly might be disregarded, and the shares of Corporation B, accordingly, could not be voted. In the absence of such proof, however, it seems clear that the shares could be voted.

[33] *Mills* v. *Williams*, 11 Ired. (N. Car.) 658.

Legal Status of Joint-Stock Associations [1]

A joint-stock company is a type of business organization which stands midway between the partnership, on the one hand, and the corporation, on the other hand. In many instances, however, it is to-day no easy matter to distinguish the unincorporated joint-stock company from the corporation, since by statutory enactment many of the most characteristic capacities and attributes of corporations have been conferred upon joint-stock associations.[2] So true is this that a learned judge has said that "the idea that these companies occupy some undefined and undefinable ground midway between a partnership and a corporation has practically faded away." [3]

At common law, a joint-stock association was a group of individuals organized for certain purposes into an association similar to a partnership but, unlike a partnership, having a capital stock, di-

[1] Fordham Law Review, Vol. 3 (1916).
[2] Clark on Corps. (3d ed.) pp. 22–25. As to the difference between the corporation and the partnership, see opinion of Cullen, Ch. J., in *Drucklieb* v. *Harris*, 209 N. Y. 211, 216.
[3] O'Brien, J., in *Hibbs* v. *Brown*, 190 N. Y. 167, 82 N. E. 1108.

vided into shares transferable by the owner.[4] Partners, the courts held, might associate themselves in a joint-stock company with transferable shares.[5] A joint-stock association in the early days was really simply a large partnership possessing some of the characteristics and powers of the private corporation.[6] In fact, except to the extent that remedial legislation has altered the rule, joint-stock associations are still subject to the principles of law relating to common-law copartnerships.[7]

The distinction between corporations and joint-stock associations is not a mere academic one. The question is at times a momentous one to answer. For example, joint-stock companies are not always liable for taxes under a statute which imposes a tax upon "corporations."[8] In order to avoid this result, statutes are so phrased to-day as to embrace within their purview both corporations and joint-stock

[4] *Attorney General* v. *Mercantile Marine Ins. Co.*, 121 Mass. 524; *Wells* v. *Gates*, 18 Barb. (N. Y.) 554; *People* v. *Coleman*, 133 N. Y. 279, 31 N. E. 96; *Hedge & Horn's Appeal*, 63 Pa. St. 273.

[5] Lindley on Company Law (6th ed.), p. 193.

[6] *People* v. *Rose*, 219 Ill. 46, 76 N. E. 42.

[7] *Hoadley* v. *Essex County Com'rs*, 105 Mass. 519; *Wells* v. *Gates*, 18 Barb. (N. Y.) 554.

[8] *Liverpool Ins. Co.* v. *Massachusetts*, 10 Wall. (U. S.) 566.

associations.[9] The facility in doing business is substantially the same in both forms of organization, and it is this facility or advantage which it is the purpose of the taxing statute to assess.[10] Again, joint-stock companies are exempt from the effect of a constitutional provision requiring corporations to be created only under general laws or requiring a two-thirds vote of the state legislature for the creation of corporations.[11]

Sometimes the legislature confers upon joint-stock associations so many attributes of a corporation that judges have differed as to the legal status of the type of organization.[12] In a comparatively recent case,[13] Judge O'Brien of the Court of Appeals of New York regarded the Adams Express Company, which is a large joint-stock association, as a "quasi corporation," saying: "A joint-stock association, whatever else may be said about it, is certainly for most, if not for all practical purposes, a legal entity capable in law of acting and assuming legal obliga-

[9] *Eliot* v. *Freeman*, 220 U. S. 178, interpreting Federal Corp. Tax Law (Act Cong. Aug. 5, 1909, c. 6, § 38, 36 Stat. 112); *Roberts* v. *Anderson*, 226 Fed. 7, 141 C. C. A. 121.

[10] *Eliot* v. *Freeman*, *supra*.

[11] *Thomas* v. *Dakin*, 22 Wend. (N. Y.) 9; *Warner* v. *Beers*, 23 Wend. (N. Y.) 103.

[12] Clark on Corps. (3d ed.) pp. 24–5.

[13] *Hibbs* v. *Brown*, 190 N. Y. 167, 82 N. E. 1108.

tions quite independent of the shareholders." And, in the same case, Judge Hiscock said: "A great association like the Adams Express Company is very unlike an ordinary copartnership and it has assumed for ordinary practical purposes in its business and contractual relations, the features and characteristics of a corporate creation, whereby the joint aggregate entity has been made prominent, and the individual units composing it have been overshadowed and obscured." On the other hand, Judge E. T. Bartlett declared in the same case: "It is unnecessary to point out in detail the very great difference between the joint-stock association and a corporation," and Judge Werner said: "The company is concededly not a corporation although our statutes have invested it with certain corporate attributes."

The federal courts regard corporations as citizens under Article III, sec. 2, of the Constitution of the United States, conferring jurisdiction upon the federal courts over controversies between citizens of different states.[14] They refuse, however, to regard joint-stock companies as citizens for pur-

[14] *Louisville R. Co.* v. *Letson*, 2 How. (U. S.) 497; *Marshall* v. *Baltimore R. Co.*, 16 How. (U. S.) 314; *Doctor* v. *Harrington*, 196 U. S. 579.

poses of federal jurisdiction.[15]   Where the bill alleged that the Adams Express Company was a joint-stock company duly organized and existing under the laws of the state of New York and a citizen of that state, and that the defendant was a citizen of the state of Missouri, the federal court in a recent case directed that the suit be dismissed for want of jurisdiction, saying: "The averment that the complainant is a joint-stock company, is not equivalent to the statement that it is a corporation." [16]

If the legislature confers upon an association all the essential attributes of the corporate body, it thereby creates it a corporation, and it would seem immaterial that the term "corporation" is not used.[17] If the legislature declares that the association shall not be a corporation, no matter how conclusive this may be in the domestic jurisdiction, it does not bind foreign jurisdictions or prevent their courts from inquiring into the true character of the association whenever that may come in issue.[18]

[15] *Great Southern Fireproof Hotel Co.* v. *Jones*, 177 U. S. 449; *Thomas* v. *Board of Trustees*, 195 U. S. 207; *Gregg* v. *Sanford*, 65 Fed. 151, 12 C. C. A. 525; *Rountree* v. *Adams Express Co.*, 165 Fed. 152, 91 C. C. A. 186.

[16] *Rountree* v. *Adams Express Co., supra.*

[17] Clark on Corporations (3d ed.), p. 15.

[18] *Liverpool Ins. Co.* v. *Massachusetts*, 10 Wall. (U. S.) 566.

Its attributes, as well as the intention of the domestic legislature, determine its status abroad.[19]

Formation.—Joint-stock companies, unlike corporations, may be formed by a mere agreement of association among the members. A joint-stock company with transferable shares is valid at common law, and will not be held illegal unless it can be shown to be of a dangerous character.[20] To-day, joint-stock companies frequently derive from a statutory source further qualities or benefits not existing at common law. Such statutory authority is not at all essential, however, to the existence of the joint-stock company, which is absolutely legal at common law. The statutory authority simply confers rights and privileges which no unincorporated association, as such, enjoys at common law.[21]

Dissolution.—A partnership may be dissolved at any time without the consent of the state, and the same rule applies to joint-stock companies except in

[19] *Liverpool Ins. Co.* v. *Massachusetts, supra; Edwards* v. *Warren Linoline & Gasoline Works*, 168 Mass. 564, 47 N. E. 502; *Tide Water Pipe Co.* v. *Assessors*, 57 N. J. L. 576, 31 Atl. 220.

[20] *Roberts* v. *Anderson*, 226 Fed. 7, 141 C. C. A. 121. And see Lindley on Company Law (6th ed.), pp. 193 *et seq.*

[21] *Roberts* v. *Anderson, supra.*

so far as it may be modified by statute.[22]   In this respect joint-stock companies differ from corporations.

Continuity of Existence.—The element of *delectus personæ* is characteristic of a partnership, and the death of a partner or the transfer of his interest *ipso facto* dissolves the partnership.   The precise opposite is true in the case of a corporation, which is unaffected by the death of a stockholder or the transfer of his shares.   In this respect, the joint-stock company resembles the corporation rather than the partnership, since the demise or withdrawal of an associate in a joint-stock company does not dissolve it.[23]   However, the right to transfer shares in a partnership business may by agreement be incorporated even into partnership articles.

Common Name.—Like corporations, joint-stock companies are known by a common name.   This does not make the body a corporation and, as is well known, partnerships are often commonly known by a trade name under which they carry on their business.[24]

[22] *Mann* v. *Butler*, 2 Barb. Ch. (N. Y.) 362.
[23] *Gleason* v. *McKay*, 134 Mass. 419; *Hibbs* v. *Brown, supra*.
[24] *Warner* v. *Beers*, 23 Wend. (N. Y.) 103.

Agency.—Each partner is an agent of the firm. On the other hand, a stockholder in a corporation is not an agent of the corporation, which acts through its duly constituted board of directors and officers. In this respect, again, a joint-stock company resembles a corporation. Joint-stock companies conduct their business through their boards of trustees or directors; their members, as such, have no power to bind them. This circumstance of resemblance does not make a joint-stock association a corporation.[25]

Contracts.—Each and every member of a joint-stock company is liable upon the contracts entered into by it.[26] Under some statutes an action may even be brought in the first instance against the individual members of the association.[27] It is more generally provided, however, that an action cannot be brought against the individual members of the joint-stock association until after judgment and execution unsatisfied against the association.[28] In this regard, a joint-stock association is more similar to a partnership than to a corporation, since

[25] *Warner* v. *Beers, supra.*

[26] *Tappan* v. *Bailey*, 4 Metc. (Mass.) 529; *Kingsland* v. *Braisted*, 2 Lans. (N. Y.) 17.

[27] See opinion of Hiscock, J., in *Hibbs* v. *Brown*, 190 N. Y. 167, 82 N. E. 1108.

[28] *Hibbs* v. *Brown, supra.*

the contracts of a corporation are the contracts of
the legal entity, and of it alone, and are not, in any
sense, the contracts of the individual members of the
corporation.[29]

Acquisition and Transfer of Property.—Except
as modified by statute, a joint-stock company, unlike
a corporation, cannot acquire and convey property
by its common name. Title must be taken and conveyed by the members as individuals. Property
may also be taken and conveyed by an officer in
trust for the members.[30] It is not necessary that an
unincorporated association should have statutory
authorization to have its real estate held by its
president (or other officer) as a trustee for its members.[31] Indeed, in a case decided recently by the
Supreme Court of the United States, the property of
an unincorporated joint-stock company was held by
trustees, and it was conceded by the court that
its right in this regard was not derived from any
statute.[32]

[29] *Bank of Augusta* v. *Earle*, 13 Pet. (U. S.) 519, at p. 587;
Erickson v. *Revere Elevator Co.*, 110 Minn. 443, 126 N. W. 130.
[30] *Pratt* v. *California Min. Co.*, 24 Fed. 869; *Byam* v. *Bick-
ford*, 140 Mass. 31.
[31] *Roberts* v. *Anderson*, 226 Fed. 7, 141 C. C. A. 121.
[32] *Eliot* v. *Freeman*, 220 U. S. 178.

Actions.—In the case of the joint-stock company, the rule at common law is that it cannot sue or be sued in the name of the association or of its officers, but must sue or be sued in the name of all of the members composing it, however numerous they may be. All are necessary parties at the common law.[33] The hardship and inconvenience of making all the members of large unincorporated associations parties to actions soon led to important remedial legislation both in England and in this country.[34] This legislation provides that such associations may sue and be sued in the name of a designated officer as, for example, the president or treasurer of the company. This officer, for the purposes of suit, is regarded substantially as the company, as distinct from the individuals composing it. Such statutes, however, do not make joint-stock associations corporations.[35] On the other hand, if all other corpo-

[33] *Roberts* v. *Anderson, supra; Van Aernam* v. *Bleistein,* 102 N. Y. 355; *Hybart* v. *Parker,* 4 C. B. (N. S.) 209.

[34] See *Roberts* v. *Anderson, supra.* In New York, the Act of 1849 authorized joint-stock companies to sue and be sued in the name of the president or treasurer. This was followed by similar legislation. The provisions are still in force, being included in the Joint Stock Association Law (Consol. Law. c. 29) [now the General Associations Law.] See, also, Constitution of New York, Article VIII, sec. 3.

[35] *People* v. *Coleman,* 133 Mass. 279, 31 N. E. 96; *Van Aernam* v. *Bleistein,* 102 N. Y. 355.

rate attributes are conferred upon the association, the mere fact that it sues and is sued in the name of an officer rather than in its artificial name should not be held to prevent the courts from treating the company as a corporation. The result is, in effect, the same, for process would have to be served on some officer even if the suit were brought in the artificial name.[36] It must be noted that suits may never be brought by or against a joint-stock company in its artificial name unless this is expressly authorized by statute.[37]

Actions by Members Against Joint-Stock Associations.—A corporation may sue its stockholders or be sued by them, and under some statutes it is held that a joint-stock company is so similar to a corporation that an action may be brought by a member against the officer designated by statute as the representative of the association, and vice versa.[38] The Constitution of New York (Article VIII, sec. 3.) expressly provides that the term "corporation" shall include joint-stock com-

[36] *Liverpool Ins. Co.* v. *Massachusetts*, 10 Wall. (U. S.) 566.

[37] *Van Aernam* v. *Bleistein, supra.*

[38] *Hibbs* v. *Brown, supra*, opinion of Hiscock, J., citing Code Civ. Proc. §§ 1919–1924 (now General Associations Law, §§ 12–16).

panies, and, accordingly, joint-stock companies
have the right to sue, and are subject to be sued,
in all cases just like corporations. Under provisions of this nature it is plain that joint-stock
companies for most practical pupuses are constituted corporations.[39] There is a clear recognition of the joint-stock association as an entity
recognized by the law as something quite distinct
and separate from its individual members.

Transfer of Shares.—The capital of a joint-
stock company unlike that of a partnership, but
like that of a corporation, is divided into shares
which are apportioned among the members in
proportion to the respective amounts which they
have dedicated to the common enterprise. These
shares are assignable by their owners like shares
of corporate stock. The right to transfer shares
in a partnership business may by agreement be
inserted into articles of copartnership, however,
and it follows that this attribute of transferabil-
ity of shares does not make a joint-stock association a corporation.[40] In the case of certain types
of joint-stock companies, *e. g.*, the Pennsylvania

[39] *Hibbs* v. *Brown, supra.*

[40] *Gleason* v. *McKay*, 134 Mass. 419; *Warner* v. *Beers*, 23
Wend. (N. Y.) 103.

JOINT-STOCK ASSOCIATIONS

"partnership association," the transferee will not become an associate unless the consent of the other members is given, either antecedently in the articles of association, or at the time of the transfer, or subsequently.[41]

Individual Liability of Members.—Unless it is provided to the contrary by statute, or by a provision in the articles of association which has been brought to the attention of creditors, the associates in a joint-stock company are personally liable for its debts.[42] The stockholders in a corporation are not liable for the debts of the corporation; the debts are regarded as those of the corporate entity and of it alone. On the other hand, partners are liable for the debts of a partnership. Joint-stock companies have nevertheless sometimes been regarded as corporations for all practical purposes, even though their members do not possess the important corporate attribute of limited liability.[43] Even corporations

[41] *Edwards* v. *Warren Linoline & Gasoline Works*, 168 Mass. 564, 47 N. E. 502; *Sheble* v. *Strong*, 128 Pa. St. 315; *Eliot* v. *Himrod*, 108 Pa. St. 569.

[42] *Pettis* v. *Atkins*, 60 Ill. 454; *Wells* v. *Gates*, 18 Barb. (N. Y.) 554; *Kingsland* v. *Braisted*, 2 Lans. (N. Y.) 17; *Frost* v. *Walker*, 60 Me. 468.

[43] *Hibbs* v. *Brown*, 190 N. Y. 167, 82 N. E. 1108.

may exist, under charter or statutory provision, where the members do not enjoy a restricted liability, without making the association any the less a corporation. It was held that, under the constitution and laws of the state of New York, the United States Express Company, a joint-stock association, was "for all practical purposes a corporation," even though its individual associates were liable for the debts of the company.[44] The statutes and constitution endowed joint-stock associations with so many corporate characteristics, and with so many capacities and attributes not in possession of a partnership at common law, that the decision was quite correct. On the other hand, the common-law liability on the part of members of joint-stock associations may be removed by statute, or by provision brought home to the notice of creditors, without thereby creating the association a corporation.[45]

The distinction between corporations and joint-

[44] *Hibbs* v. *Brown, supra,* opinions of Hiscock, J., and O'Brien, J.

[45] *Warner* v. *Beers*, 23 Wend. (N. Y.) 103. See, also, *Andrews Bros. Co.* v. *Youngstown Coke Co.*, 86 Fed. 585, 30 C. C. A. 293. The authority of the last cited case is shaken, if in fact the decision is not overruled, in *Great Southern Fireproof Hotel Co.* v. *Jones*, 177 U. S. 449.

stock companies with regard to individual liability would seem to be that stockholders in a corporation are not liable for its debts unless they are expressly made liable by statute; whereas, on the other hand, the associates in a joint-stock association are individually liable for its debts unless this liability is expressly removed by statutory enactment or by agreement brought home to the notice of creditors. The creation of a corporation, so to speak, drowns out the individual liability of the members, whereas the creation of a joint-stock association has not this inherent effect unless so provided by express affirmative enactment or stipulation.[46] Individual liability for debts is, however, not a positive criterion whereby to distinguish corporations from joint-stock associations, since, as has been seen, the principle of stockholders' personal liability is not at all inconsistent with the fact of corporate existence.[47]

Merger of Associates into Artificial Personality.—We have seen that a joint-stock company is not a corporation simply because it is authorized by the state, or because its shares are transferable, or

[46] *People* v. *Coleman*, 133 N. Y. 279, 31 N. E. 96.
[47] And see Clark on Corporations (3d ed.), pp. 20, 24.

because it has an artificial name, or even because its associates may not be personally liable for its debts. It has been suggested that the distinguishing mark between a joint-stock company and a corporation is whether the association exists as a legal entity distinct and separate from the associates as individual persons; if there is such separate entity and artificial personality, then the body is a corporation, otherwise it is a joint-stock company.[48] The difficulty with this is that it is begging the question to assert that the body is a corporation if it be a legal entity, since, in order to determine whether the body is a legal entity, it is first necessary to consider the legislative intent and the attributes conferred upon the body.

In a well-known New York case,[49] Judge Finch suggested that the distinction is "that the creation of the corporation merges in the artificial body and drowns in it the individual rights and liabilities of the members, while the organization of a joint-stock company leaves the individual rights and liabilities unimpaired and in full force." This suggestion is not satisfactory, for associations have

[48] *Andrews Bros. Co.* v. *Youngstown Coke Co.*, 86 Fed. 585, 30 C. C. A. 293, opinion *per* Lurton, J.

[49] *People* v. *Coleman*, 133 N. Y. 279, 31 N. E. 96.

JOINT-STOCK ASSOCIATIONS

frequently been held by the courts to be corporations, though the members are by charter made individually liable for the debts of the body. The
principle of stockholders' personal liability is not
necessarily inconsistent with the fact of corporate
existence,[50] and as said by Mr. Justice Miller, speaking for the Supreme Court of the United States,
"it is quite certain that the principle of personal
liability of the shareholders attaches to a very large
proportion of the corporations of this country and
it is a principle which has warm advocates for its
universal application when the organization is for
pecuniary gain." [51]   The Court of Appeals of this
state, however, has never altogether abandoned its
position that the distinguishing feature of the joint-
stock association, as contrasted with the corporation, is the personal liability of its members; and,
indeed, this feature of personal liability has been regarded by some members of the court as so co-
existent with the life of the joint-stock association
that it cannot be abrogated even by the contract
of the parties in interest.[52]

[50] See note 47, *supra*.

[51] *Liverpool Ins. Co.* v. *Massachusetts*, 10 Wall. (U. S.)
566.

[52] *Hibbs* v. *Brown*, 190 N. Y. 167, 82 N. E. 1108, opinions of
Cullen, Ch. J., Edward T. Bartlett, J., and Werner, J.

Conclusion.—The truth is, in fine, that the modern joint-stock association, as the result of statute, is so frequently endowed with most of the familiar attributes of the private corporation that to-day it is a matter of the greatest difficulty in many instances to determine precisely where the legal domain occupied by joint-stock associations begins and ends. The so-called "partnership association" of the state of Pennsylvania is recognized in that state as a body quite distinct from a corporation,[53] and it is so treated in some of the states, for example, in Massachusetts.[54] On the other hand, other states regard it as a corporation, insisting that the essential attributes of the body are those of a corporate entity and that, therefore, it is a corporation.[55] These latter states insist that the true test is not so much what the legislature intended to do as what the legislature has really done, and that a legislature actually can create a corporation although not intending to do so.[56]

[53] *Sheble* v. *Strong*, 128 Pa. St. 315; *Eliot* v. *Himrod*, 108 Pa. St. 569.

[54] *Edwards* v. *Warren Linoline & Gasoline Works*, 168 Mass. 564, 47 N. E. 502.

[55] *Tide Water Pipe Co.* v. *Assessors*, 57 N. J. L. 576, 31 Atl. 220; *Edgeworth* v. *Wood*, 58 N. J. L. 463, 33 Atl. 940.

[56] See Clark on Corps. (3d ed.) pp. 14 *et seq.*

JOINT-STOCK ASSOCIATIONS

The difficulty is that oftentimes the legislature has not clearly in mind exactly what it intends to do, with the result that the courts are burdened with questions of statutory interpretation and construction which are as tantalizing as they are unnecessary. The problem should be squarely confronted. The statutes of the different states, particularly New York and Pennsylvania, on the subject of joint-stock associations should be redrafted so as to define more precisely the legal status of the bodies created thereunder. This course would at least do away with the absurdity of the present situation, when no two judges of the self-same court are fully agreed upon what a joint-stock association is in the eye of the law.[57] The only alternative to this suggested legislative drafting of a scientific statute is to do away entirely hereafter with the joint-stock association as a type of business organization, and to confine trading groups to the partnership and the corporation. This would have the positive merit of drawing a horizontal line across the list of trading groups, confining corporations to its lower side and partnerships to its upper side, and thereby eliminating the illogical and confusing twilight zone now present.

[57] *Hibbs* v. *Brown*, 190 N. Y. 167, 82 N. E. 1108.

Power of a Corporation to Acquire Its Own Stock [1]

THERE are two general views of corporate capacity. The first view regards a corporation as possessed of general capacity, by which is meant that the corporation may do anything that a natural person can do, unless the act is either expressly or impliedly prohibited by its charter.[2] This theory has met with little favor in the United States. In this country, the doctrine of special corporate capacity has been almost universally adopted.[3] Under this view, a corporation possesses only the powers conferred upon it in its charter, together with those powers which are incidental to, or consequential upon, or reasonably necessary for effectuating the main powers conferred. And in the case of the ordinary private corporation, American courts

[1] Yale Law Journal, Vol. 24 (1915).

[2] *South Yorkshire R. Co.* v. *Great Northern R. Co.*, 9 Exch. 84. But see *Ashbury Railroad Carriage & Iron Co.* v. *Riche*, L. R. 7 H. L. 653.

[3] *Thomas* v. *West Jersey R. Co.*, 101 U. S. 71; *Franklin Bank* v. *Commercial Bank*, 36 Oh. St. 350.

are inclined to take a liberal view of its powers, inclining more and more to hold that if the sovereign state does not intervene, there is no valid reason for confining the operations of the ordinary private corporation too closely.[4]

Implied powers are presumed to exist to enable corporate bodies to carry out the express powers granted, in order adequately to accomplish the purposes of their creation. Suppose no express power is conferred upon a corporation to acquire its own shares. The question arises whether the corporation may make such a purchase or whether it is outside of and beyond the limit of its powers. Perhaps on no subject in the law of corporations is there more conflict of authority.[5]

At the outset it seems necessary to distinguish two much abused terms, namely, "Power" and "Right." Much difficulty arises from the unfortunate use by courts of the term "Power." In the last analysis, a corporation has *power* to do almost anything. The question is not so much whether it has the *power* to do the act, as whether it has the *right* to do the act. A and B enter into a contract. A assuredly has the *power* to break the

[4] See *Harris* v. *Independence Gas Co.*, 76 Kans. 750.
[5] 27 Harv. Law Rev. 747; 14 Col. Law Rev. 451.

agreement, but that does not give A the *right* to break it. Suppose a corporation is organized to purchase and sell groceries at retail. It has the *might*, it has the *power*, but surely not the *right* to purchase and operate a circus and menagerie. Yet, courts speak illogically of the want of corporate *power* to purchase the circus and menagerie. The terminology misleads and confuses. There can be no question but that a corporation has the *power* to acquire its own shares. No well considered case in any jurisdiction should question this. The issue is solely one as to the *right* of the corporation to do so.

On the question of right, there exist two lines of decisions. One line enunciates what may be termed the English rule; the other what may be termed the American rule. The English view regards the purchase as *ultra vires*, unless the corporation has been expressly authorized to buy its own shares. The leading case of *Trevor* v. *Whitworth* [6] assigns two main reasons for this conclusion. First, it is said that if the corporation acquires its shares with a view to selling them again, this is an unauthorized speculation in its own stock,

[6] 12 Appeal Cases, 409. And see *Hope* v. *International Financial Society*, 4 Ch. Div. 327.

TO ACQUIRE ITS OWN STOCK

amounts to a trafficking in its shares, and is *ultra vires*. On the other hand, if it is not intended to reissue and part with the shares, then the purchase amounts to an invalid and unauthorized reduction of its own capital stock. It is insisted that the dilemma is perfect, and that in either event the purchase of its own stock is unlawful. Quoting Lord Herschell:

> "What was the reason which induced the company in the present case to purchase its shares? If it was that they might sell them again this would be a trafficking in the shares, and clearly unauthorized. If it was to retain them, this would be to my mind an indirect method of reducing the capital of the company."

Neither of these reasons is altogether convincing. Nobody would question the right of a corporation to sell shares of its own stock which it acquired, for example, by gift [7] or by bequest.[8] Nobody would question the right of a corporation to part with shares of its own stock which it had taken in payment of an antecedent indebtedness.[9] Yet, this, too, would be trafficking in the corporation's own shares. Under a reasonably fair

[7] *Lake Superior Co.* v. *Drexel*, 90 N. Y. 87.

[8] *Rivanna N. Co.* v. *Dawson*, 3 Gratt. (Va.) 19.

[9] *Coppin* v. *Greenless & Ransom Co.*, 38 Oh. St. 275.

123

POWER OF A CORPORATION

(not liberal) view of corporate powers,[10] there seems
no adequate reason for objecting to this in the
absence of facts and circumstances tending to
show fraud or impropriety. With regard to the
argument that the purchase is an indirect method
of reducing the corporate capital stock, it is a
sufficient answer to point out that the purchase
is not necessarily a reduction.[11] The shares are
simply retired for the time being and may be re-
issued at will. Quoting Judge Danforth of the
Court of Appeals of New York:[12]

> "In some way it (the corporation) had be-
> come the owner of these shares, not for the pur-
> pose of diminishing its capital stock, but for
> enjoyment as property. As such they stood
> upon its books, until in the regular transaction
> of business the stock was transferred to Conk-
> ling. The company had a right to hold it *un-
> extinguished*, and a right to *reissue* it."

[10] As to what is the appropriate test for construction of
implied powers, see the opinion of Vice-Chancellor Bacon in
London Financial Assn. v. *Kelk*, 26 Ch. Div. 107, 134.

[11] *Western Imp. Co.* v. *Des Moines Nat. Bk.*, 103 Iowa, 455;
City Bank of Columbus v. *Bruce*, 17 N. Y. 507; *State* v. *Smith*,
48 Vt. 266; *Howe Co.* v. *Jones*, 21 Tex. Civ. App. 198. In
this regard, Morawetz, and Machen who follows Morawetz,
seem to err. Morawetz, Priv. Corps. (2d ed.), § 112;
Machen, Modern Law of Corps., § 626. And see 27 Harv.
Law Rev. 748-9, for a correct appreciation of the situation.

[12] *Vail* v. *Hamilton*, 85 N. Y. 453, 457-8.

TO ACQUIRE ITS OWN STOCK

This also answers the contention of the authorities and text writers who insist that a purchase
by a corporation of its own shares is an unlawful
method of reducing the capital stock, not being
the method provided for by law.[13] The flaw in
the argument lies in the assumption that a purchase of its own shares must necessarily involve a
reduction of capital stock.

Another argument advanced in support of the
English doctrine is that the purchase of its own
stock by a corporation operates necessarily as a
fraud upon creditors who deal with the corporation on the faith that the capital stock is paid up.[14]
A recent text writer [15] thus voices it:—

> "It is no answer to say that if the company
> is thoroughly solvent, so that its assets after
> the purchase are still amply sufficient for pay-
> ment of all claims against it, the creditors are
> not prejudiced. For, while the assets may still
> remain sufficient, yet they are after the con-
> summation of the purchase, undeniably less by
> the amount of the purchase money than they

[13] Thus see M'Sherry, C. J., in *Maryland Trust Co.* v.
Nat. Mech. Bk., 102 Md. 608, especially 623–6.

[14] *Trevor* v. *Whitworth, supra; Maryland Trust Co.* v. *Nat.
Mech. Bk., supra;* 2 Thomp., Corps., § 2054 (erroneous "trust
fund" argument).

[15] Machen, Modern Law of Corps., § 626.

were before; and hence the fund which the creditors had an *absolute right* to have preserved intact for the payment of their claims, has been diminished without their consent."

This argument involves several fallacies. Suppose no creditors exist. Then, of course, the argument fails utterly. If there are no creditors, how can creditors be injured? Suppose, however, that there are creditors, but the purchase of its own shares is made from a goodly *surplus* which the company has been accumulating.[16] Surely nobody would contend that the corporate surplus is a fund "which its creditors had an *absolute right* to have preserved intact for the payment of their claims." That creditors must be injured by the corporate purchase of its own stock does not necessarily follow, and consequently the rights of creditors furnish no conclusive argument in support of the English doctrine. If creditors are injured by such a purchase, they can be amply protected without going to the extreme—quite unnecessary in order to protect them—of denying

[16] See *Hamor* v. *Taylor-Rice Engineering Co.*, 84 Fed. 392: "Was the money which the defendant undertook to pay him for his surrender of stock to come out of any surplus or fund of net profits, on the one hand, or on the other, out of the fund represented by the capital stock?"

to a corporation the right ever to acquire its own shares.[17]

It is also urged that to permit a corporation to acquire its own shares results unjustly, since it increases the relative voting strength of large stockholders and results in giving undue power to the majority.[18] If no fraud or bad faith on the part of the majority appears, this argument fails completely, and it is elementary that if fraud or bad faith do appear, the minority may obtain ample and adequate relief.[19] If abuse results, the abuse should be stifled. But the corporation should not be unduly hampered by laying down the arbitrary rule of non-acquisition of its own shares, irrespective of good or bad purpose, object and result.

Finally, the argument has been made that, viewed from the theoretical standpoint, the acquisition by a corporation of its own shares is anomalous. "It is inconsistent with the essential nature of a company that it should become a member of itself." [20] And it is insisted that is precisely

[17] *Clapp* v. *Peterson*, 104 Ill. 26.

[18] Machen, Modern Law of Corps., § 626.

[19] As to powers of majority and rights of minority, see Canfield & Wormser's Corporation Cases (1st ed.), 704-26. See, also, *Lowe* v. *Pioneer Threshing Co.*, 70 Fed. 646.

[20] *In re Dronfield Silk Stone Co.*, 17 Ch. Div. 83. For a

what a corporation does when it acquires its own
stock.[21]   Whatever validity this argument may
have, the courts following the English doctrine
seem estopped to assert it, since all of them permit a corporation to take over its own stock in
satisfaction of a debt due to it.[22]   In such instances,
the theoretical inconsistency is ignored by them,
perhaps upon the assumption that necessity knows
no law,—a practical view, but a trifle illogical.

In the United States, several jurisdictions, including Kansas, Maryland, Missouri, New Hamp-
shire, Ohio and Tennessee, follow the English doctrine and deny that the right to acquire its own
shares should be implied as a corporate power.[23]
National banks are forbidden by express statute
to buy their own shares.[24]   In England, "the Stock

similar Continental point of view, see H. Staub, Kommentar
zum Handelsgesetzbuch (7th ed.) I, p. 679.

[21] *Maryland Trust Co.* v. *Nat. Mech. Bk.*, 102 Md. 608,
623–6.

[22] See Canfield & Wormser's Cases, (1st ed.), 214, note.

[23] *German Sav. Bk.* v. *Wulfckubler*, 19 Kans. 65; *Maryland
Trust Co.* v. *Nat. Mech. Bk.*, 102 Md. 608; *St. Louis Carriage
Mfg. Co.* v. *Hilbert*, 24 Mo. App. 338; *Currier* v. *Lebanon Slate
Co.*, 56 N. H. 262; *State* v. *Oberlin Bldg. & Loan Assn.*, 35
Oh. St. 258; *Cartwright* v. *Dickinson*, 88 Tenn. 476.   In many
cases cited as supporting the English doctrine, including some
of the above, the language is *obiter.*

[24] Rev. St. U. S., § 5201.

Exchange will not grant a settling day, or allow a quotation to any company which purports to have the power of buying its own shares." [25] In Germany, the Commercial Code (§ 226) forbids private corporations from acquiring their own shares either in the course of business or in pledge. Shares may not even be purchased out of surplus. The only exception is where the purchase of shares is necessary to carry out plans of retirement or amortization. Even this must have been stipulated for in the articles of association.[26] The motive of the German provision has been regarded as twofold: "First, because it is repugnant to legal concepts that a corporation be its own shareholder, and secondly, because the provision tends to prevent speculation in the shares of the corporation by its officers and managers, who might thus obtain unfair advantages on the credit of the organization." [27]

In England and in American jurisdictions which follow the English view, an exception to the rule

[25] *Per* Lord Macnaghten in *Trevor* v. *Whitworth, supra.*

[26] German Comm. Code, § 227. And even then, the purchase may only be made out of the corporate surplus.

[27] Kuhn, A Comparative Study of the Law of Corporations, p. 123 (Columbia Univ., Studies in History, Economics and Public Law, Vol. XLIX, No. 2).

POWER OF A CORPORATION

that a corporation cannot traffic in its own stock,
is admitted to exist, whereby the corporation is
allowed to take its own stock as collateral,[28] or to
effect a compromise of a disputed claim against a
stockholder,[29] or in satisfaction of a debt due to
the corporation.[30] "This exception is supposed
to rest on a necessity which arises in order to avoid
loss." [31] It seems proper to say that several early
cases only held this limited proposition, but have
been apparently used as authorities for the broad
proposition of a general right to acquire. Thus,
in *Taylor* v. *Miami Exportation Company*,[32] it was
held in Ohio that a banking corporation might
lawfully receive shares of its own stock from a
solvent debtor in discharge of his indebtedness.
In the early New York case, *City Bank of Columbus*
v. *Bruce*,[33] it appeared that the board of directors
of a banking corporation passed a resolution that

[28] *Williams* v. *Savage Mfg. Co.*, 3 Md. Ch. 452.

[29] *State* v. *Oberlin Bldg. & Loan Assn.*, *supra; Morgan* v.
Lewis, 46 Oh. St. 1.

[30] *First Nat. Bk.* v. *Nat. Exch. Bk.*, 39 Md. 600; *Maryland
Trust Co.* v. *Nat. Mech. Bk.*, *supra; Taylor* v. *Miami Exp.
Co.*, 6 Oh. 176; *Coppin* v. *Greenless & Ransom Co.*, 38 Oh.
St. 275, 279; *Morgan* v. *Lewis*, *supra*.

[31] McIlvaine, J., in *Coppin* v. *Greenless & Ransom Co.*, *supra*.
[32] 6 Oh. 176.
[33] 17 N. Y. 507.

all stockholders indebted to the bank on stock notes might pay such debts to the bank in its shares of stock at a named percentage, and that almost one-half of the stock of the bank was so surrendered. The Court of Appeals held, following the Ohio case, that there was "no ground for questioning the validity of this transaction." These two cases, at a later day, seem to have been used as authority in support of much more than they actually hold.[34]   Even national banks may take shares of their own stock "to prevent loss upon a debt previously contracted in good faith." [35]

The general American rule, in support of which is the decided weight of authority, affirms that a corporation has implied power to take its own shares, provided it does so in good faith and without an injury to its creditors or stockholders.[36]

[34] Thus see *Chicago, etc., R. Co.* v. *President, etc., of Marsellles*, 84 Ill. 643. *Cf.* Angell & Ames, Corps., § 280.

[35] Rev. St. U. S., § 5201.

[36] *Dalton Grocery Co.* v. *Blanton*, 8 Ga. 809; *Clapp* v. *Peterson* 104 Ill. 26; *Dupee* v. *Boston Water Power Co.*, 114 Mass. 37; *Porter* v. *Plymouth Gold Mining Co.*, 29 Mont. 347; *Chapman* v. *Iron Clad Rheostat Co.*, 62 N. J. L. 497 (statutory provision); *City Bank of Columbus* v. *Bruce, supra; Vail* v. *Hamilton, supra; Moses* v. *Soule*, 63 Misc. Rep. (N. Y.) 203, 118 N. Y. Supp. 410; *Adam* v. *New Eng. Inv. Co.*, 33 R. I. 193; *San Antonio Co.* v. *Sanger*, 151 S. W. (Tex. Civ. App.) 1104; *State* v. *Smith*, 48 Vt. 266; *U. S. Mineral Co.* v. *Camden*, 106.

POWER OF A CORPORATION

The underlying reason for the American doctrine, as it may be termed, seems to be the feeling on the part of most American courts that the English doctrine is far too narrow and rigid and unduly ignores customary business demands. Thus, under the doctrine of England, as has been seen, a purchase by a corporation of its own shares is *ultra vires*, (1) Even though *bona fide;* (2) Even though all the stockholders consent; (3) Even though there is no defrauding of, or intent to defraud, creditors.

The American doctrine, however, carefully safeguards the exercise of this right. As said by the Supreme Court of Illinois:—[37]

> "If it was shown that the purchase was made to promote the interests of the officers of the company alone, and not the stockholders generally, or if for the benefit of a portion of the stockholders and not all, or for the injury of all or only a portion of them, or if operated to the injury of creditors, or would defeat the end for which the body was created, or if it was done for any other fraudulent purpose, then chancery could interfere."

Va. 663; *Gilchrist* v. *Highfield*, 140 Wis. 476; *In re Castle Braid Co.*, 145 Fed. 224. See, also, *Chicago, etc., R. Co.* v. *President, etc., of Marseilles*, 84 Ill. 643, for a review of the early authorities.

[37] *Chicago, etc., R. Co.* v. *President, etc., of Marseilles, supra.*

TO ACQUIRE ITS OWN STOCK

The American doctrine fully recognizes that
the exchange of corporate property or cash for
shares of its own stock, and canceling the stock,
furnishes no equivalent for creditors. It must not
be supposed that this is not recognized, for it is.
The purchase must be in good faith and will only
be upheld provided it is made without intent to
injure creditors and stockholders and provided
they are not, in fact, injured thereby.[38]

Some of the criticism leveled at the prevailing
doctrine apparently seems based upon the assumption that the corporate majority may vote the
shares acquired. The law, however, is well settled
that a corporation may not vote shares of its own
stock held by it, either directly, or indirectly through
a trustee.[39] Suppose Corporation A acquires all
the shares of stock of Corporation B; suppose
Corporation B acquires ten shares of stock in Corporation A; may Corporation B, through its ac-
credited agent for that purpose, vote the ten shares
of stock which it owns in Corporation A at a meeting of the stockholders of Corporation A? Is this
a voting by Corporation A of its own shares of

[38] *Clapp* v. *Peterson, supra.*

[39] *Amer. R. Frog Co.* v. *Haven,* 101 Mass. 398; *Ex parte
Holmes,* 5 Cow. (N. Y.) 426. See, also, Cook, Corps. (7th
ed.), § 613.

POWER OF A CORPORATION

stock? It seems clear that on principle, Corporation B should have the right to vote its ten shares, under the prevailing and orthodox entity doctrine. Corporation B is a distinct and separate legal personality and juridical body from Corporation A. *Non sequitur*, if Corporation B were organized or the stock transfers made, solely in order to attain certain desired voting results, that the veil of entity might not be pierced, especially if an improper or fraudulent purpose appeared. It must not be supposed that the doctrine of corporate entity can be employed as a species of legal whitewash.[40]

Several situations present themselves under the prevailing American doctrine. First, suppose the contract of purchase is made and payment completed while the corporation is solvent. Under such circumstances, on principle it should be held that even though insolvency *thereafter* ensues, the trustee in bankruptcy should not be permitted to recover the corporate payments.[41] Even in jurisdictions which follow the English doctrine, the con-

[40] See paper, "Piercing the Veil of Corporate Entity," 12 Columbia Law Rev. 496 *et seq*.

[41] *Joseph* v. *Raff*, 82 N. Y. App. Div. 47, aff'd short, 176 N. Y. 611. See, also, *Tierney* v. *Butler*, 144 Iowa, 553.

tract of purchase, although *ultra vires*, being consummated, should not be disturbed. On the other
hand, in the very few jurisdictions which hold that
it is not only *ultra vires* but *illegal* and *against public
policy* as well for a corporation to acquire its own
shares, the contract though fully consummated
seemingly may be repudiated and the consideration
recovered back.[42]   The distinction between re-
garding the purchase as *ultra vires* and as *illegal*
is obvious.[43]   Suppose a corporation organized to
run a retail groceries business contracts to purchase two performing elephants. By no stretch of
the human imagination could this be called an
illegal act, an act *contra bonos mores*. At most,
the purchase is simply unauthorized, that is to
say, *ultra vires*.

Second, suppose the contract is made when the
corporation is insolvent.   Under such circumstances, the purchase is clearly invalid, under
either the English or the American doctrine, since
it jeopardizes the capital stock and diminishes the

[42] *Crandall* v. *Lincoln*, 52 Conn. 73. *Sed qu.*

[43] But the Supreme Court of the United States seems to have
overlooked this distinction.   Thus see, *Central Transporta-
tion Co.* v. *Pullman's Palace Car Co.*, 139 U. S. 24; *St. Louis,
Vandalia & Terre Haute R. Co.* v. *Terre Haute & Indianapolis
R. Co.*, 145 U. S. 393. And so have many other authorities.

fund to which creditors would naturally look.[44] On elementary principles of the law of fraud, the transaction should be vitiated.

Third, suppose the contract of purchase is made when the corporation is solvent, but the payment of the purchase price for the shares would cause insolvency. This transaction also should be condemned; and the contract regarded as unenforceable since fraudulent to creditors.[45] The creditors of a corporation which is being wound up, and who have a natural right to look to paid-up capital as the fund out of which their debts are to be discharged, should not be forced to come into competition with stockholders in the company who claim that the company is bound to pay them a part of the capital. The transaction is inchoate and the court should not be forced to compel its completion.

Fourth, suppose the contract of purchase is made when the corporation is solvent, but the corporation becomes insolvent before payment is made or completed. Here again, the transaction

---

[44] *Hall* v. *Alabama, etc., Co.*, 173 Ala. 398; *Tiger Bros.* v. *Rogers, etc., Co.*, 96 Ark. 1; *Alexander* v. *Relfe*, 74 Mo. 495; *Currier* v. *Lebanon Slate Co.*, 56 N. H. 262.

[45] *Atlanta Assn.* v. *Smith*, 141 Wis. 377. See, also, 2 Va. Law Rev., at p. 74. *Cf. Trevor* v. *Whitworth, supra.*

TO ACQUIRE ITS OWN STOCK

is inchoate. This situation was considered by the
United States Circuit Court of Appeals for the
Second Circuit, in a learned decision.[46] A New York
corporation while solvent purchased certain shares
of its own stock giving a note for the purchase
price. When the note given in payment matured,
the corporation was insolvent. It was held unanimously that payment of the note should be post-
poned until after the claims of general creditors
had been satisfied. In other words, if, at the time
the stockholder is to receive payment for the shares
of stock which he has sold, the payment by the
corporation would prejudice its creditors, payment cannot be enforced. On principle and as a
common-law proposition this holding is sound,
since in no jurisdictions, English or American,
should a corporation ever be permitted to consummate a purchase of its own shares where this
might work a detriment or injustice to creditors.
Even though the corporation is solvent when the
agreement is made, the law should attach the condition that payment cannot be enforced if to enforce payment would deprive the creditors of assets.

Judge Rogers, in his opinion, found it unneces-

[46] *In the Matter of Fechheimer Fishel Co., Bankrupt,* 212
Fed. 357 (1914), opinion *per* Rogers, J.

137

sary to pass upon the case as a common-law proposition because of the express statutory provision
in New York, which declares guilty of a misde-
meanor any directors who vote "to apply any
portion of the funds of a corporation, except surplus profits, directly or indirectly, to the purchase
of shares of its own stock." (Penal Law of New
York, § 664, subd. 5.) Quoting from the opinion:

> "But we are not by any means to understand
> that a corporation has a right to buy its own
> stock, simply because it is solvent at the time,
> because if it becomes insolvent thereafter and
> before payment has been made, or if it is made
> insolvent by the transaction, the payment can-
> not be made, for the Penal Law of the State
> makes it a crime to apply anything but 'surplus
> profits' to the purchase of the stock and there
> are no such profits which can be applied."

One recent criticism of the decision [47] fails to refer
to the statutory prohibition upon which the decision is rested. Another [48] doubts "that the legislature intended by a provision contained in the
penal law to impose such a limitation upon the
power of the corporation as delineated in the corporation law." This criticism fails to cite, ap-

[47] 27 Harvard Law Rev. 747–50.
[48] 14 Columbia Law Rev. 451.

138

TO ACQUIRE ITS OWN STOCK

parently overlooking, the decision of the Court
of Appeals of New York upon the applicability of
this provision.[49]   The action therein was brought
upon a contract made by a corporation to purchase
its own stock.   The action was defended by the
corporation upon the ground that the contract
was not enforceable by reason of the provisions
of § 664 of the Penal Law, making it a mis-
demeanor for directors to apply any of the funds
of a corporation, except surplus profits, to that
purpose.   The court held that the burden of proof
was upon the corporation of showing that there
were no surplus profits out of which the purchase
could be made.   It is obvious that the court assumed that the purchase of shares of its own stock
out of capital stock would be improper.   The
Court of Appeals said:—

> "The contract itself, therefore, was perfectly
> legal, subject to certain limitations upon its
> enforceability.   *If when the time came it had a
> sufficient surplus, the contract would be enforced.*"

It follows that certainly under the New York
statute, as interpreted by the New York courts,
if not indeed as a common-law proposition, the

[49] *Richards* v. *Ernst Wiener Co.*, 207 N. Y. 59 (1912), aff'g
145 App. Div. 353.

POWER OF A CORPORATION

federal decision is sound. Its tendency is commendable, since jurisdictions which permit a corporation to acquire its own stock should, and do, carefully safeguard the rights of creditors as primary and supreme.[50]

One factor overlooked by many decisions dealing with this subject is the practical distinction, as obvious to business men as it should be to the courts, and plainly recognized by the New York statute, between a purchase of its own shares by a corporation out of *capital*, and a similar purchase out of *surplus*. Where the purchase is made from surplus, it is difficult to see how creditors can be injured, and if the corporation as a whole is benefited by the purchase, there seems no valid reason for forbidding the directors to employ the corporate surplus in this manner.[51]

On principle, a purchase by a private corporation

[50] *Clapp* v. *Peterson, supra.* But *cf. Cole* v. *Cole Realty Co.*, 169 Mich. 347.

[51] See *Lowe* v. *Pioneer Threshing Co.*, 70 Fed. 646 (*Semble*); *Clark* v. *E. C. Clark Machine Co.*, 151 Mich. 416. In *Hamor* v. *Taylor-Rice Engineering Co.*, 84 Fed. 392, the burden of proof was placed upon plaintiff, the vendor, to show a surplus. *Cf. Richards* v. *Ernst Wiener Co., supra*, where the New York court held the burden to be upon the corporation, the vendee, to prove that there was no surplus out of which the purchase of its shares could lawfully be made.

of its own shares from surplus should be upheld by the courts,

(1) Provided a legitimate and proper corporate object is advanced.

(2) Provided the condition of corporate affairs warrants it.

(3) Provided the transaction is designed and carried out in entire good faith.

(4) Provided the corporation receives full and clear value.

(5) Provided there is intended and there results no undue advantage to a few favored stockholders at the expense of the remainder.

(6) Provided the rights of creditors are not jeopardized.

If the rights of creditors and the rights of stockholders are thus safeguarded, and if purchase be permitted from surplus alone as distinguished from capital stock, there would seem no valid reason for denying to a corporation the right to acquire shares of its own stock.[52] On the contrary, to deny the right under such conditions and circumstances, would unduly hamper corporate activity and usefulness and the serviceability of the private corporation as a type of business organization.

[52] See *Price* v. *Pine Mt. Iron Co.*, 32 S.W. (Ky. Ct. App.) 267.

Legality of Corporate Voting Trusts and Pooling Agreements [1]

T HE inclination of the early authorities was to condemn all attempts to tie up a majority of the stock of a corporation by a surrender on the part of stockholders of their voting power, and both voting trusts and pooling agreements were frowned upon as illegal.[2]

The tendency of rules of law, however, is to follow economic and industrial necessities. This is especially true in the law of private corporations, and, to the credit of the courts, in general they have responded in an elastic and willing manner so as to

[1] Columbia Law Review, Vol. 18 (1918).

[2] Two typical cases are *Bostwick* v. *Chapman* (1890), 60 Conn. 553, 24 Atl. 32 (Shepaug Voting Trust Cases); *Harvey* v. *Linville Improvement Co.* (1896), 118 N. C. 693, 24 S. E. 489. In the last cited case, Clark, J., a distinguished jurist, said, at p. 699: "In short all agreements and devices by which stockholders surrender their voting powers are invalid. 5 Thompson Corporations, § 6604. The power to vote is inherently annexed to and inseparable from the real ownership of each share, and can only be delegated by proxy with power of revocation." *Griffith* v. *Jewett* (1886), 15 Wkly. Law Bul. (Ohio) 419; also, paper by Ex-Judge Simeon E. Baldwin 1 Yale Law Journal, 1, *Accord.*

TRUSTS AND POOLING AGREEMENTS

adjust corporate conceptions to economic and social facts and developments.[3]   Accordingly, in the course of time, the courts came to recognize the desirability of sanctioning voting trusts and pooling agreements whereby the control of the corporation might be secured for the support of a continuous policy of management, or for the development of a sound method of administration of corporate affairs, or for the successful working out of a reorganization plan.

For example, suppose a majority of the stockholders of a corporation desire to work in harmony in order to establish and develop a certain continuing corporate policy.   Such a result might be achieved, perhaps, by an agreement between stockholders to vote together.   Or, better still, it might be achieved through an agreement by which proxies are given to certain trustees with power to vote the proxies as they may be directed or may determine. Or, best of all, through an agreement by which the legal title to the stock is transferred to the trustees with power to vote thereon.[4]   When the stockholders, or a portion of them, transfer their shares of stock

[3] See, "Piercing the Veil of Corporate Entity," 12 Columbia Law Rev. 496, 517–8.

[4] Clark, Corporations (3d ed.), 600.

to the voting trustees, the voting trustees acquire the legal title to the stock and the right to vote the stock, but the stockholders retain the other incidents of beneficial ownership of the stock, and, in return for their stock, trust certificates are given to them, which certificates are ordinarily transferable, just like stock certificates, subject, however, to the terms and conditions of the voting trust agreement.

Again, let us suppose a case where a corporation has fallen into financial straits and the bondholders or their committee are in a position to compel a foreclosure sale. This may occur in cases even where the corporation is solvent but is unable to maintain its interest payments. It stands to reason that the bondholders will not consent to a reorganization of the corporation (and refrain from foreclosure) unless they are given some definite assurance that, in the immediate future, careful management and proper voting control will be insured. The security holders are vitally interested in seeing that a sound, logical and continuing corporate policy will be adopted, which will insure and protect their safety. In order to work out the reorganization of the corporation, it is necessary also to give assurance to the bondholders that men of financial standing and high integrity are to be in charge of the corporate enterprise for the initial period in the future. Under these circumstances, it is clear that the use of the voting trust is most desirable, until such time, at least, when the theoretical security of the bond-holders has become actual security. Besides this, the financial interests which undertake the work of reorganization are also interested in seeing that a suitable management is assured in the reorganization of the corporation, since the bankers' own reputations are involved. An unsuccessful reorganization would injure the standing of the bankers. It follows that financial interests would be unwilling to undertake the financing of the work of reorganization unless the continuity and integrity of the control are assured, and this can be achieved most readily and simply through the simple device of the corporate voting trust.

The courts, bearing in mind these practical considerations, had gradually come, for the most part, to sustain the legality of the voting trust agreement, and by the year 1905 or thereabouts, the decided weight of legal authority had come to recognize that there was nothing illegal or contrary to public policy in separating the voting power of the stock from its beneficial ownership.[5]

[5] *Smith* v. *San Francisco, etc., Ry.* (1897), 115 Calif. 584, 47

LEGALITY OF CORPORATE VOTING

In some jurisdictions the legality of the voting trust had even obtained statutory recognition. Thus, in New York, in 1892 and 1901, the legislature enacted the following statute, which is now § 25 of the General Corporation Law.[6]

> "A stockholder may, by agreement in writing, transfer his stock to any person or persons for the purpose of vesting in him or them the right to vote thereon for a time not exceeding five years upon terms and conditions stated, pursuant to which such person or persons shall act; every other stockholder, upon his request therefor, may, by a like agreement in writing, also transfer his stock to the same person or persons and thereupon may participate in the terms, conditions and privileges of such agreement; the certificates of stock so transferred shall be surrendered and canceled and certificates therefor issued to such transferee or transferees in which it shall appear that they are issued pursuant to such agreement and in the entry of such

Pac. 582; *Brightman* v. *Bates* (1900), 175 Mass. 105, 55 N. E. 809; *Boyer* v. *Nesbitt* (1910), 227 Pa. 398, 76 Atl. 103. In these cases the authorities generally are collected and adequately summarized.

[6] Laws of 1892, c. 687, § 20; Laws of 1901, c. 355, § 1 (now Gen. Corp. Law, § 25). [This section has now been modified. The term, for instance, is now ten years. (N. Y. Stock Corp. Law, § 50.)]

TRUSTS AND POOLING AGREEMENTS

> transferee or transferees as owners of such
> stock in the proper books of said corpo-
> ration that fact shall also be noted and
> thereupon he or they may vote upon the
> stock so transferred during the time in such
> agreement specified; a duplicate of every
> such agreement shall be filed in the office
> of the corporation where its principal busi-
> ness is transacted and be open to the in-
> spection of any stockholder, daily, during
> business hours."

In Maryland, a similar statute was enacted in
1908.[7]

In 1900, Chief Justice Holmes of Massachusetts,
now Mr. Justice Holmes, said:[8]

> "We know nothing in the policy of our law
> to prevent a majority of stockholders from
> transferring their stock to a trustee with
> unrestricted power to vote upon it."

In the same year, 1900, the New Jersey Court of
Chancery said:[9]

---

[7] Md. Laws of 1908, c. 240.

[8] *Brightman* v. *Bates, supra,* footnote 5, at p. 111. See, also,
Elger v. *Boyle* (1910), 69 Misc. Rep. 273, 126 N. Y. Supp.
946, a valuable opinion by the late Justice Bischoff.

[9] *Chapman* v. *Bates* (1900), 61 N. J. Eq. 658, 666–7, 47
Atl. 638; *cf. Warren* v. *Pim* (1904), 66 N. J. Eq. 353, 59 Atl.
773 (in this case the court was divided seven to six, and it is
submitted that the dissenting opinion by Swayze, J., is
the sound one).

147

LEGALITY OF CORPORATE VOTING

> "There is no statutory provision, nor can
> we perceive any reason offensive to pub-
> lic policy, preventing a stockholder from
> giving another powers over, or rights in,
> his shares in a corporation to the same ex-
> tent that he might give in any property."

In 1910, the Supreme Court of Virginia, in commenting upon the cases which discuss the validity
of voting trusts and pooling agreements, said: [10]

> "In considering the cases, however, and
> the text-writers who have commented upon
> them, it is impossible not to be impressed
> with *the change of opinion which has taken
> place with respect to the true nature of such
> contracts.* In the early stages of the devel-
> opment of this idea there was a strong sen-
> timent against them which found expres-
> sion in the opinions of judges and in the
> not always temperate language of distin-
> guished commentators upon the law; *but
> experience has demonstrated their usefulness,
> and the hostility evinced toward them has by
> degrees diminished.*"

In the years 1912–13, as they now appear in their
proper perspective, a crusade began against the use
of the voting trust or pooling agreement. The
Pujo Committee of 1913, in its report to the House

[10] *Carnegie Trust Co.* v. *Security Life Ins. Co.* (1910), 111 Va.
1, 20, 68 S. E. 412. The italics are ours.

148

of Representatives, severely condemned voting trusts, and submitted that they should be regarded as illegal *per se*, irrespective of their purposes, objects, or intentions. The committee took the view of the early decisions, declaring broadly that the power to vote should be deemed inseparable from the beneficial ownership of the stock and that any agreement or device by which the stockholders combined to place the voting power of their shares of the stock in other persons, *e. g.*, voting trustees, is illegal and against sound public policy. It should be remarked that no evidence had been introduced *pro* and *con* before the committee, for the purpose of determining whether, in general, voting trusts have been a benefit or a detriment, and whether voting trusts, whose propriety and just purpose appear, should be condemned.[11]

Mr. Samuel Untermyer, the counsel for the committee, at about the same time, condemned voting trusts in vivid language.[12]

---

[11] Cushing, Voting Trusts, 23 (a valuable treatise).

[12] Untermyer, A Legislative Program, 25. Since then, Mr. Untermyer has also condemned what he terms "the vice of proxy voting," and suggests "the abolition of proxy voting." Untermyer, The Lawyer-Citizen—His Enlarging Responsibilities (a paper read at the annual meeting of the Commercial Law League, July 27, 1916).

LEGALITY OF CORPORATE VOTING

This agitation was not without its effect upon the courts, and the decisions reflect its effect and consequences. At least two courts have adopted a point of view, as a result, which is unprogressive and reactionary, although it may reflect the popular whim and caprice of the passing moment.

In *Luthy* v. *Ream*,[18] the Supreme Court of Illinois, in 1915, had occasion to consider the validity of a voting trust of stock of the Peru Plow & Wheel Company, a corporation of the state of Illinois. The effect of the voting trust agreement, entered into by the majority of the stockholders of the company, was to place the legal title of the majority of the stock in one Ream, as voting trustee, who was given the power to vote the stock for a term of ten years upon all questions and at every meeting of the stockholders, according to his discretion. It was provided that, at all elections of directors of the company, the voting trustee should nominate three directors to be voted for at such election, and should vote all of the stock held by him as a unit for each and all of the directors so nominated by him. Some time subsequently, some of the stockholders sold their shares, and their vendee presented the

---

[18] (1915) 270 Ill. 170, 110 N. E. 373.

trust certificate for the stock and demanded that a stock certificate should be issued for the shares of stock represented thereby. The corporation refused to issue such stock certificate, stating that the shares of stock were included in the trust agreement, and that it could not and would not issue a new stock certificate to the vendee for that reason. Whereupon, the vendee notified the corporation that, as owner of the shares in question, he withdrew them from the trust agreement and would no longer be bound thereby, and demanded that a stock certificate be issued to him free from any restraint, obligation or condition under such trust agreement.

It should be further noted that, after the sale of the shares in question, Ream, as voting trustee, no longer represented a majority of the stock, but only a minority.

The question was thus squarely presented to the court as to the legal validity of the voting trust agreement and the right of a stockholder, who was a party thereto, to withdraw therefrom within the time specified therein.

The Supreme Court of Illinois had previously held in several cases that it was legitimate and legal for the owners of a majority of the stock of a corporation to combine for the purpose of controlling the corporation.[14] In this *Luthy* case, however, the court held that the voting trust agreement was illegal and void, and that the holder of the voting trust certificate must be allowed to revoke the voting trust agreement, so far as he is concerned, at any time. This is a return to the point of view of the early decisions. It is a self-styled "progressive" point of view. It may be a popular point of view, but it is unsound logically, contrary to business needs and demands, and therefore, in truth, a reactionary and unprogressive point of view. The court's main argument was that it is unsound public policy for stockholders to be permitted to divest themselves personally of the right to vote for a term of years and to confer the right to vote upon their trustees. Quoting from the opinion:[15]

> "The voting power of the stock is absolutely separated from its ownership for a term of years, so that the real owners of the property are during that time entirely divested of its management and control or of any participation therein. Our law contemplates that corporations shall be controlled by a majority of the stockholders

[14] *Faulds* v. *Yates* (1870), 57 Ill. 416; *Venner* v. *Chicago City Ry.* (1913), 258 Ill. 523, 101 N. E. 949.

[15] *Luthy* v. *Ream, supra,* footnote 13, at pp. 177–8, 180. The italics are ours.

acting through directors elected by them
in person or by proxy, and it has been held
that a by-law of a corporation which authorizes bondholders to vote for directors
at stockholders' meetings is in violation
of both the constitutional and statutory
provisions requiring directors to be elected
by a majority of the shares of stock of the
corporation. (*Durkee* v. *People*, 155 Ill.
354.) *The power to vote for directors can be
exercised only by stockholders in person or
by proxy, and they cannot be deprived or deprive themselves of this power. Stockholders cannot evade the duty imposed upon them
by law of using their power as stockholders
for the welfare of the corporation and the general interest of its stockholders.* A stockholder may refuse to exercise his right to
vote and participate in stockholders' meetings, but he cannot deprive himself of the
power to do so.

*   *   *   *   *

"A stockholder may ordinarily withdraw from a combination to control the
majority of the stock of a corporation
and a contract not to transfer his shares
to the opposition or vote against the combination, although it is expressly agreed
that the contract shall be irrevocable."

This is an argument which might very properly
be addressed to a legislative tribunal, but which has
no place in a court of law, and in particular, it has

no place in a court which had hitherto held that stockholders have a common-law right to vote by proxy, even in the absence of statutory authorization.[16]

The Illinois court cited several early cases, including the early Shepaug Voting Trust Cases in Connecticut.[17] It then reached the following conclusion.[18]

> "The principle to be deduced from these cases is that the holders of the majority of the shares of stock in a corporation may control its management, and every person who becomes an owner of stock has a right to believe that the corporation will, and to insist that it shall, be managed by the majority; *that the power to vote is inherently attached to and inseparable from the real ownership of each share, and can only be delegated by proxy, with power of revocation;* that each stockholder must be free to cast his vote, whether by himself or by proxy, for the best interest of the corporation, and that each stockholder has the right to demand that every other stockholder, if he desires to do so, shall have the right to exercise at each annual meeting his own judg-

[16] *People ex rel. Chritzman* v. *Crossley* (1873), 69 Ill. 195.

[17] *Bostwick* v. *Chapman, supra,* footnote 2.

[18] *Luthy* v. *Ream, supra,* footnote 13, at p. 181. The italics are ours.

ment as to the best interest of all the stockholders, untrammeled by dictation, and
unfettered by the obligation of any contract."

The Illinois court, furthermore, expressly repudiated the sound decision of the Supreme Court of
California in *Smith* v. *San Francisco & North Pacific
Railway Co.*,[19] in which case it was held that an
agreement by several purchasers of stock in a corporation to vote it as a unit for five years, in accord-
ance with the decision of the majority, is binding
upon the parties and irrevocable. It also disapproved the decision of the Supreme Court of
Virginia in *Carnegie Trust Co.* v. *Security Life
Insurance Co. of America*,[20] in which case it was held
that an agreement among stockholders to place
their stock in the hands of voting trustees for
twenty-five years to enable the trustees to manage
the corporation, constitutes a valid trust. The
decision of the Supreme Court of Illinois in the
Luthy case marks a reversal of the court's own policy
as indicated in its earlier decisions, although the
court professed to be able to distinguish the earlier
Illinois cases. The essence of the holding seems to
be that the court believes that the power to vote
stock is annexed to and inseparable from the bene-

[19] *Supra*, footnote 5.　　　[20] *Supra*, footnote 10.

ficial ownership of each share of stock, and can be delegated only by revocable proxy. In fact, the language of the Supreme Court of Illinois, above quoted, is identical (though not quoted) with that used in an early decision in North Carolina.[21]

In the next year, 1916, a proposed plan of reorganization of the St. Louis & San Francisco Railroad Co. was presented to the Public Service Commission of the State of Missouri by J. & W. Seligman and Company and Speyer and Company, the reorganization managers. One provision of the plan, termed the "voting trust," under which it was proposed that the stock of the reorganized company should be held and voted by certain trustees for a period of five years, read as follows:[22]

> "The preferred and common stock of the New Company (except such number of shares as may be disposed of to qualify directors) shall be vested in the following voting trustees: Frederic W. Allen, George W.

[21] See language of Clark, J., in *Harvey* v. *Linville Improvement Co.*, *supra*, footnote 2, with which compare the language of Dunn, J., in *Luthy* v. *Ream*, *supra*, footnote 13.

[22] *In re St. Louis & S. F. R. R. Reorganization* (1916), 3 Mo. Pub. Ser. Comm. 664, at p. 707.

TRUSTS AND POOLING AGREEMENTS

Davison, Seward Prosser, Charles H. Sabin, James Speyer, Frederick Strauss and Festus J. Wade.

"In the event of the death or failure or refusal to serve of any person designated as a voting trustee prior to the creation of the voting trust, the vacancy shall be filled by the reorganization managers. The stock shall be held by the voting trustees, and their successors, jointly (under a trust agreement prescribing their powers and duties and the method of filling vacancies), for five years, although the voting trustees may, in their discretion, deliver the stock at an earlier date. Until delivery of stock is made by the voting trustees, they shall issue certificates of beneficial interest entitling the registered holders to receive, at the time therein provided, stock certificates for the number of shares therein stated, on payment of any taxes in connection with the surrender of voting trust certificates and the transfer and delivery of stock certificates, and in the meanwhile to receive payments equal to the dividends collected by the voting trustees upon the number of shares therein stated, which shares, however, with the unrestricted voting power thereon, shall be vested in the voting trustees until the stock shall be delivered, as provided in the trust agreement and in the voting trust certificates issued thereunder."

LEGALITY OF CORPORATE VOTING

The reason for making this voting trust scheme a part of the plan of reorganization was stated by one of the reorganization managers, as follows: [23]

> "Q. What special reasons were there for a desire on the part of the present bondholders to place the stock in a voting trust?
>
> "A. The refunding bondholders and general lien bondholders, both, naturally felt that they should have a voice in the management of the property when they were asked to make sacrifices for the benefit of the stock and for the benefit of the property generally. The refunding 4s had the biggest part of the total bond issue of eighty-five million dollars. They took instead only three-quarters of the principal in the new four-per-cent bond, the rest being taken as a contingent charge, and the issue of which they were asked to have a part is now raised to $250,000,000. They felt as they were enlarging the amount of the mortgage and providing for the future capital of this road, that they were making a sacrifice of a fixed interest-bearing obligation, in part at least, for a contingent one, and that they should have a voice in the property. The same thing applies with even greater force to the general liens because they were still taking a

[23] At p. 708.

> greater part of their principal in contin-
> gencies, contingent charges, so we thought
> the fairest way to do would be to take two
> representatives from each of the three im-
> portant classes of securities, the two bonds
> and the stock and apportion that stock
> representation partly east and partly west
> as the stock is held partly in the east and
> partly in the west, and then appoint a
> seventh man in the manner I have just
> described.
>
> "It was thought that Mr. Allen (sev-
> enth member) would represent in an ad-
> mirable manner the eastern part of his
> own firm and eastern investors on the one
> hand and in a measure also the west."

It thus appears that four of the seven trustees
named were selected to represent the bondholders,
two to represent the stockholders, and one to be
"regarded as a sort of neutral." Bearing in mind
that the bondholders were vitally interested, because of the sacrifices which they were making for
the benefit of the railroad property, and for the
general good, it would seem that the reorganization
plan was just and reasonable.

The Public Service Commission of Missouri,
however, relying upon the early Shepaug Voting
Trust Cases,[24] held "that the voting trust pro-

[24] *Bostwick* v. *Chapman*, *supra*, footnote 2.

vided for in the plan of reorganization is against
the public policy of this State." [25] Accordingly,
it was rejected as invalid and void. Subsequently,
the personnel of the trustees was changed, and an
application was made to the commission for a re-
hearing and reconsideration. The commission
stated that the change of trustees did not relieve
the voting trust of its objectionable features, saying: [26]

> "The serious objection to the voting
> trust feature of the original plan of reor-
> ganization was that it placed the selection
> of the voting trustees, and consequently
> the election of the board of directors and
> the management and control of the com-
> pany, in the hands of the bondholders in-
> stead of the stockholders, as provided by
> the Constitution and law of this State.
> The modified plan now considered pro-
> poses the substitution of the two names of
> voting trustees in lieu of two named in the
> original plan, but makes no change what-
> ever as to the method of the selection of
> the trustees. It is apparent that a change
> of trustees does not relieve the voting
> trust of the objectionable feature to which

[25] At p. 712.
[26] *In re St. Louis & S. F. R. R. Reorganization, supra,*
footnote 22, Supplemental Report of the Commission, at pp.
720–1.

attention was called in the former opinion. The Commission did not object to
the personnel of the trustees first named,
but rather to their selection by the bondholders, and as to that feature no change
has been made in the plan as modified."

The commission, accordingly, again disapproved
the voting trust provision submitted in the plan of
reorganization.

It thus appears that the agitation and crusade
of the years 1912–13 were not without their effect
upon the courts. The Supreme Court of the state
of Illinois, we find, practically reversed itself, and
we find the Public Service Commission of the state
of Missouri taking a similar positive and unquali-
fied position in opposition to the validity of the
voting trust or pooling agreement. This attitude
was taken in spite of the fact that the federal court
for the southern district of New York, in working
out a dissolution plan of the New Haven Railroad,
itself created voting trusts consisting of three
sets of trustees, each consisting of five members,
a circumstance of much significance, since the
voting trusts were created by the express mandate
of the federal judiciary.

On sound principle, it is submitted that there
is nothing about voting trusts which should cause

courts to hold them illegal *per se*. It is submitted, on the contrary, that each and every argument urged against the validity of voting trusts is specious.

It has been urged that each holder of shares is entitled to the personal judgment and to the personal vote of all the shares. This is the argument of the Shepaug Voting Trust Cases, adopted recently, as we have seen, by the Supreme Court of Illinois and by the Public Service Commission of Missouri, and approved by the courts of North Carolina. Mr. Untermyer takes the same position.[27] From a practical standpoint, this argument amounts to nothing, because of the huge size of modern corporations. Is it feasible to hold a mass meeting of ten thousand stockholders? Is it practicable to hold a mass meeting of the ninety thousand stockholders of the Pennsylvania Railroad Company? Is it possible to obtain an army cantonment wherein to assemble the legions who constitute the stockholders of the United States Steel Corporation? This very practical consideration nullifies the argument that every stockholder is entitled "to the judgment of each individual stockholder." When it is said that the stockholder of a corporation is entitled to the bene-

[27] See footnote 12, *supra*.

TRUSTS AND POOLING AGREEMENTS

fit of the judgment of each and every other stockholder in the management of the corporate affairs, it cannot be meant, moreover, that a stockholder is entitled to hamper in any way the free
and honest exercise of the judgment of his fellow-
stockholders. Each stockholder may act as he
chooses. It follows that the question is whether
it is unlawful to contract to do what it is perfectly
lawful to do. Why cannot stockholders, consist-
ently with sound public policy, in order to secure
a reorganization of their corporation, and the
securing of a necessary loan, vest the management
of the corporation in hands satisfactory to the
banking interests, which lend the money, and for
a term commensurate with the loan? Again, why
cannot a group of stockholders combine for a
term of years and make their union effective by
means of the simple device of a voting trust?
A trust may be created of any other kind of personal property, and why not, therefore, of shares
of stock? It is nothing short of foolish for a court
or for a jurist to speak of the "obligation" of stockholders to assemble together at the time of a corporate election. Under modern conditions, this
is as unreasonable as it is impossible in many cases.
But in spite of these hard, practical considerations,

altruistic visions and ideals of stockholders' meetings similar to New England town meetings are still indulged and persisted in by some courts.

It has also been urged that voting trusts are invalid *per se* because they suspend the power of alienation. There seems little in this objection. In almost every known instance of voting trusts, there is no period when the outright conveyance of the stock may not legally and validly be made.

The Supreme Court of Illinois has urged, following the early cases, that the voting power should not be separated from the stock ownership and argues that, therefore, voting trusts are illegal. In the first place, this argument is based upon an unsound premise, because in the case of most voting trusts, the voting power follows the legal ownership of the stock. The legal title to the stock is in the voting trustees, and they have the power to vote it. In the second place, why cannot a stockholder give another person a power over, or right in, his shares of stock in a corporation in the same way and to the same extent that he might give rights in any other personal property?

It has also been urged that voting trusts are mere "dry trusts" and, therefore, stockholders may revoke them, though they are in form irrevocable. In the case of most voting trusts, however, the trust is an active one. Besides, as suggested by Chief Justice Holmes, "It might be held that the duty of voting incident to the legal title made such a trust an active one in all cases." [28] The doctrine as to dry trusts, therefore, does not apply in these cases.

It has also been objected that the voting trust is a method of trying to evade the statutory rule, which usually exists, forbidding the creation of proxies for longer than a certain given term. The answer to this contention is very simple. The voting trust is not a mere proxy, but is a change of legal title in and to the stock. It is an outright conveyance of the stock, conditioned upon certain covenants made by the voting trustees and certain duties imposed upon them.

The argument has also been advanced that voting trusts are undemocratic." [29] This is the "public policy" argument in another form. It is readily answered. A majority of individual stockholders may be destroyed at any moment,

[28] *Brightman* v. *Bates, supra,* footnote 5, at p. 111.
[29] See paper by Ex-Judge Simeon E. Baldwin, 1 Yale Law Journal, 1, 15.

LEGALITY OF CORPORATE VOTING

provided that a single interest buys a sufficient amount of stock. The unit of corporate control is the *share of stock*, rather than the *individual stockholder*. A majority means a majority in interest, not in number. Moreover, this objection is met by the terms of most voting trusts, which provide that any other stockholder may participate in the terms, conditions and privileges of the voting trust agreement; and in New York this is expressly provided for in the statute, adopted also in Maryland, which regulates the subject of voting trusts and pooling contracts.

Thus it appears that voting trusts should not be held illegal *per se*. Even a number of the cases which hold particular voting trusts to be invalid, usually recognize the proposition that there may be a valid voting trust.[30]

It is submitted that, on sound principle, voting trusts and pooling agreements should be upheld as valid and legal, provided that the propriety of their object and the good purpose of their creation affirmatively appear. In other words, the voting trust should not be condemned *per se*. The validity of the trust should be made dependent upon

[30] See *Kreissl* v. *Distilling Co. of Am.* (1900), 61 N. J. Eq. 5, 47 Atl. 471.

TRUSTS AND POOLING AGREEMENTS

the purposes for which the trust is created, the
powers that are conferred, and the propriety of
the objects in view. If the pooling, or combining,
or trust is designed to carry out a particular corporate policy with a view to promote the best
interests of the corporate body of stockholders,
the agreement should be upheld as valid. On the
other hand, where the voting trust or pooling
agreement is created to consummate an unfair
or monopolistic purpose, it should be condemned.

Many apparently conflicting decisions are re-
concilable under this test and when the purposes
of the voting trust or pooling agreement in each
particular case are scrutinized carefully. As said
in 1912 by the highest court of Vermont: [31]

> "The defendant says that the agree-
> ment referred to amounts to a voting
> trust, and is therefore illegal and void.
> But this result does not necessarily fol-
> low. Such agreements are not illegal *per
> se. Their validity depends upon the pur-
> poses they are designed to observe.* Where
> these purposes are lawful, stockholders
> may, in the absence of constitutional or
> statutory restrictions, suspend for a time
> the right to vote their stock and vest it in

[31] *Thompson-Starrett Co.* v. *Ellis Granite Co.* (1912), 86 Vt.
282, at p. 289, 84 Atl. 1017. The italics are mine.

167

> others who have a beneficial interest in it
> or the corporate business,—as corporate
> creditors or a trustee for them."

And as said by the highest equity court of New
Jersey in 1900:[32]

> "whether the transaction is open to the
> objection of other stockholders, as depriv-
> ing them of the right they have to the aid
> of their co-stockholders, *must be depend-
> ent upon the purposes for which the trust was
> created, and the powers that were conferred.*"

To summarize.[33] It is unsound to hold that
"all agreements and devices by which stockholders
surrender their voting powers are invalid." It
is unsound to hold that voting trusts are void
per se, as opposed to good public policy. Such a
point of view is surely unprogressive. It ignores
business necessities. It disregards economic considerations. It shuts its eyes to business actualities.
While it is true that many of the early cases adopted
this attitude, it would be most unfortunate for

[32] *Kreissl* v. *Distilling Co. of Am., supra*, footnote 30, at
p. 14, *per* Magie, Ch. The italics are mine.

[33] This summary of the law was quoted and followed by the
Appellate Division of the Supreme Court of New York, 1st
Dept., in *Tompers* v. *Bank of America* (1926), 217 App. Div.
691, 217 N. Y. Supp. 67, reversing 126 Misc. 753, 214 N. Y.
Supp. 643, which also cited and quoted this article.

TRUSTS AND POOLING AGREEMENTS

the courts again to swing around to it. That there
is some real danger of their doing so, is illustrated
by the decisions in such powerful jurisdictions as
Illinois and Missouri.

The correct rule to adopt is to uphold the legality of the voting trust or pooling agreement, provided the propriety and reasonableness of its object affirmatively appear, and provided that the
arrangement itself is honest and equitable. The
voting trust, in other words, should not be condemned as void *per se*, but should only be condemned in those instances where the trust or pooling agreement is created and carried out in order
to effectuate an improper, unjust, or monopolistic
object. The writer submits that, in jurisdictions,
unlike New York and Maryland, where this subject is not yet regulated by statute, this course is
the sound, logical and just one for the courts to
adopt.

May the Courts Compel the Declaration of a Corporate Dividend? [1]

THE opinion in an early Louisiana case, *State v. Bank of Louisiana*,[2] intimates that if the board of directors of a corporation err in good faith in refusing to declare a dividend from surplus profits, the court would be without jurisdiction to interfere, saying through Martin, J.: "If the board honestly err in these matters, we are not ready to say the courts possess the power to rectify its mistakes." The court suggests that the remedy may be left to the stockholders, who have the power at each annual election to change the constituency of the board of directors.

In a well-known New York case, *Williams v. Western Union Telegraph Co.*,[3] the court utters a similar intimation, saying: "When a corporation has a surplus, whether a dividend shall be made, and if made, how much it shall be, and when and where it shall be payable, rest in the fair and honest

[1] Southern Law Quarterly, 1918, Vol. III, 281–92.
[2] 6 La. 745 (1834).
[3] 93 N. Y. 162 (1883).

discretion of the directors uncontrollable by the courts." The unmistakable inference is that if the discretion of the board is exercised in good faith the courts should not interpose in behalf of a shareholder.[4]

It is clear that in no event should courts of law interpose in behalf of complaining stockholders. There is no form of remedy at law. A writ of mandamus would not be proper, inasmuch as the matter of declaration of dividends is essentially discretionary with the board of directors.[5]

The plastic remedies of chancery are, however, sufficiently elastic to meet the situation, and courts of equity have repeatedly held that where the directors of a corporation have acted fraudulently or dishonestly in determining whether a dividend should be declared, they may compel the wrong-doing board to declare a dividend, since a court of chancery may decree specific performance of the duty, which rests upon the board, to exercise its discretion honestly, fairly and unoppressively.[6]

[4] *Hiscock* v. *Lacy*, 9 Misc. Rep. (N. Y.) 578, 595 (1894); 30 N. Y. Supp. 860.

[5] *Rex* v. *Governor of Bank of England*, 2 Barn. & Ald. 620. See, also, Clark on Corps. (3d ed.), p. 433.

[6] *McNab* v. *McNab & Harlin Mfg. Co.*, 62 Hun (N. Y.), 18,

In other words, there is no doubt that a court of equity will not permit directors to act dishonestly and fraudulently in refusing to declare a dividend, because directors may be regarded as quasi-trustees.

The question considered by the dicta of the Louisiana and the New York courts, above quoted, is, however, a much closer one. May courts of equity interfere with the discretion of the directors where they have acted honestly, though erroneously, in the exercise of their discretion? Both of the dicta intimate broadly that the courts are without power to rectify the errors of a board of directors which has acted honestly, although mistakenly, in determining whether a dividend should be declared.

The writer submits that these dicta are unsound. While as a succinct summary of general equity policy they are true enough, since equity is properly loath to interfere with the discretion of corporate directors who are elected by the stockholders, yet it would be most unfortunate to hold, as an absolute proposition of law, that courts of equity lack jurisdiction to compel the declaration

16 N. Y. Supp. 448, aff'd short, 133 N. Y. 687, 31 N. E. 627 (1891); *Laurel Springs Land Co.* v. *Fougeray*, 50 N. J. Eq. 756, 26 Atl. 886 (1893), rev'g. *Fougeray* v. *Cord*, 50 N. J. Eq. 185 (1892).

of a dividend where a board of directors has unreasonably and unsoundly, although honestly, refused repeatedly to distribute a great surplus
among the stockholders.

Before discussing the authorities and the distinctions made by them, it seems desirable to
point out a few controlling considerations. As a
general rule, courts refuse to have anything to do
with the internal management of private corporations for pecuniary profit. In a corporation, just
as in a republic, the majority must govern, and the
minority must submit to the mandate of the majority. Whatever may be done by the directors,
acting as prescribed by law, must of necessity be
submitted to by the minority. Corporations
could not be conducted upon any other basis. It
follows that all questions within the scope of the
corporate powers which relate to the policy of
administration of the corporation or to the ex-
pediency of proposed acts, are, in general, beyond
the province of the courts. Corporate elections
furnish the only remedy for ordinary internal
corporate dissensions.[7] The point is that not
even a court of equity with its broad jurisdiction

[7] See *Flynn* v. *Brooklyn City R. Co.*, 158 N. Y. 493, 53 N. E.
520 (1899).

and elastic remedies can be expected to run a business corporation. The directors who are chosen by the stockholders, must manage the corporation. They act on behalf of the stockholders, who choose them, and, as the Louisiana court suggestively remarks, the stockholders always have it within their power at each annual election "to change their agents." [8]

To this general proposition, however, there are some exceptions. One of the most important is that founded on fraud. A court of equity, acting upon the complaint of stockholders, can compel directors to act honestly by undoing their work if they act otherwise. It follows from this that stockholders have a clear remedy if the directors act in bad faith in refusing to declare a dividend out of surplus profits. Thus, in a New York case,[9] an action in equity was brought against the Third National Bank of Syracuse and its directors, by certain of its minority stockholders, to compel the payment of a dividend out of its surplus earnings, upon the ground that the declaration of dividends had been suddenly suspended by the management of the bank about five years previously, in bad

[8] See note 7, *supra*, and note 2, *supra*.
[9] *Hiscock* v. *Lacy*, note 4, *supra*.

faith, for the purpose not only of oppressing the minority stockholders, but at the same time of obtaining an indirect pecuniary advantage to the members of the majority, by way of excessive salaries and liberal loans. It will be noted that this was not a case involving the division of certain surplus profits of an ordinary business corporation, but a case where the minority stockholders sought to have the court order a moneyed corporation, namely, a bank, to declare a dividend. The case was elaborately argued by distinguished counsel. The subsequent Chief Judge of the Court of Appeals of New York, Honorable Frank H. Hiscock, appeared for the plaintiffs. The opinion was written by the late Judge Vann, one of the ablest jurists of the last generation in New York. The opinion points out that the persistent refusal of the directors to declare dividends, plainly suggested that they were trying to "freeze out" the minority stockholders, and indicates that the withholding of dividends depreciated the market price of the stock of the bank and tended to force the outside stockholders to sell their stock for less than it was worth. The evidence showed that there never was a time during the five years when the bank was not able to declare a dividend, and the court held that, inasmuch as it plainly appeared that the directors had acted in bad faith, and had failed to use a fair and upright discretion, a court of equity had ample power to interfere, and concluded that the bank should pay a dividend of not less than twenty per cent. The learned judge said: [10] "From the authorities cited the rule may fairly be drawn that where, without doubt, the surplus of a corporation properly applicable to a dividend is ample for the purpose, and the directors, or a majority of them, acting in bad faith, and without reasonable cause, refuse to declare a dividend, the courts will interpose in favor of these stockholders who otherwise would be without remedy."

Thus, bearing in mind that practically all courts concede that under the general equity powers a court of equity may intervene where the board of directors fraudulently, oppressively, or unfairly, refuses to declare a dividend, and may under such circumstances specifically enforce the declaration of a dividend out of the corporate surplus, we now come to the consideration of the more difficult question raised by the dicta above quoted.

The question might be thus framed:—Will the

[10] 9 Misc. Rep. at pp. 597–8.

discretion of a board of directors concerning the declaration of a dividend be interfered with by a court of equity in the absence of bad faith, of fraud, or dishonesty? In other words, suppose that the directors act entirely unreasonably in refusing to declare dividends, but that they are acting in good faith and honestly according to their conscience,— under these circumstances, under the general equity powers, may stockholders obtain the relief of specific performance in the forum of equity? Under these circumstances, may a court of equity order that done which ought to be done?

In the course of his opinion in the bank case already referred to, Judge Vann uttered a dictum very similar to those uttered by the Louisiana and New York courts, saying:[11] "Directors are not required to be wise, but they are required to be honest." If, by this statement, Judge Vann meant to intimate that courts of equity are helpless to interpose except where it appears that directors have acted dishonestly or fraudulently, or to gratify malice, or to promote their personal interests, then, it is submitted, the learned judge erred. A director must be more than a mere gilded figure-head. When he accepts the position of director, to which the stock-

[11] 9 Misc. Rep. at p. 592.

holders have elected him, he impliedly warrants not only that he is a man of honesty, but that he is a man of average prudence and ability competent to fill the office of director, and it is submitted that, where the directors of a corporation fail to show the wisdom of ordinary prudent and reasonable men, they are not relieved from liability simply because they have been personally honest.[12]

It must be conceded that there are many such dicta which, although conceding that the discretionary power of the directors is not absolute, nevertheless would deny the right to a court of equity to intervene on behalf of complaining stockholders, where there is an absence of bad faith or dishonesty on the part of the board. While courts of equity are properly loath to interfere,[13] especially where bad faith is absent, it is submitted that if the right to a dividend is clear and there are obviously ample funds from which it can properly be declared, and the board of directors has nevertheless unreasonably refused to declare a dividend, a court

[12] *Gibbons* v. *Anderson*, 80 Fed. 345 (1897); *Warner* v. *Penoyer*, 91 Fed. 587, 33 C. C. A. 222 (1898); *Rankin* v. *Cooper*, 149 Fed. 1010 (1907).

[13] See *Rollins* v. *Denver Club*, 43 Colo. 345, 96 Pac. 188, 18 L. R. A. (N. S.), 733 (1908).

of equity should intervene to compel the directors of a corporation to declare it. To order the declaration of a dividend under these facts calls for the exercise of the ordinary equity weapon of specific performance, and where it is clear that the directors have abused their discretion in unreasonably refusing to declare a dividend, a court of equity is amply warranted in ordering relief.

The mere existence of "a large amount of surplus" is not sufficient, however, to warrant intervention.[14] It must be borne in mind that the directors in the exercise of their discretion may deem it to the advantage of the corporation to expand its business, or to guard against depreciation, or to accumulate considerable surplus. Such a course of conduct might be not only provident, but often excellent business as well. But where it appears that dividends have unreasonably and unfairly been detained from distribution among the stockholders for a long period of years, a point may be reached where a court of equity should unhesitatingly intervene and direct the directors to do their duty and declare a dividend. In such a case a court of equity should set its remedial machinery in motion on behalf of

[14] *Trimble* v. *American Sugar Refining Co.*, 61 N. J. Eq. 340, 48 Atl. 912 (1901).

any dissenting stockholder who may bring a bill of complaint.[15]

Such a bill should be brought by the complaining stockholders not in their own behalf only, but also in behalf of all other stockholders who may come in and unite in the action and share in its expense.[16] In other words, the suit is an ordinary stockholders' or "representative" action, in which the corporation and its directors are joined as defendants by the complaining shareholders.

But it must always be borne in mind that, in the absence of bad faith or fraud on the part of the directors, only in a strong and extreme case will a court of equity interfere with the discretionary powers of the directors by compelling them to declare a dividend. And, if it is in this respect only that the dicta of the Louisiana and the New York courts, above quoted, are intended to be understood, then they may be regarded as correct enough, because, as a matter of general policy, courts of equity are properly most reluctant to substitute their own discretion and judgment in lieu of that of the directors, to whom the stockholders of the corporation

[15] *Stevens* v. *U. S. Steel Corp.*, 68 N. J. Eq. 373, 59 Atl. 905 (1904); see, also, Clark on Corps. (3d ed.) at pp. 426-7, and authorities there collected in notes 72-9, inclusive.

[16] 9 Misc. Rep. at p. 598.

have entrusted the obligation and the duty of determining when, where, in what amount, and in what manner dividends shall be declared from corporate surplus. Just as a trial judge should be properly reluctant to set aside the verdict of a jury of twelve men on a contested issue of fact which it is within the province of a jury to pass upon and determine, so a court of equity should be properly reluctant to interfere with the judgment of the directors of a corporation who are vested by the stockholders with a wide discretionary power in regard to the distribution of surplus profits in the form of dividends among the shareholders. It is submitted, however, that there may come a point when a court of equity should and will intervene on behalf of injured stockholders who seek redress by a representative suit in equity.

After all is said and done, the directors of a corporation should know that the only positive benefit to the stockholders to be derived from the successful prosecution of the business of the corporation must come from the distribution of dividends in cash or property. That is why stockholders acquire stock ordinarily,—in order to obtain dividends. The piling up of an immense surplus which remains undistributed, may, in the end, go solely to future creditors of the corporation, and this fact, also, the directors should realize. And, therefore, where the directors act unreasonably and unsoundly, although perhaps honestly, in refusing to declare dividends, equity intervention is, it is submitted, fully warranted.

There are two or three helpful distinctions and limitations which may profitably be considered by a court of equity in passing upon this subject in a given case. The rights of common stockholders and of preferred stockholders with reference to compelling the declaration of a dividend, do not stand upon an identical footing. While in both cases the existence of a surplus is a condition precedent to the declaration of a dividend,[17] the right of a common stockholder to dividends rests merely upon his relationship to the corporation as a stockholder, whereas the right of a preferred stockholder to dividends rests upon an agreement as well between himself and the corporation, whereby it is stipulated that in the event that profits are earned and dividends declared therefrom, he is entitled to them in a certain amount and at certain times.[18] While the obligation of a board of directors to declare divi-

[17] *Lockhart* v. *Van Alstyne*, 31 Mich. 76 (1875).

[18] See *Scott* v. *B. & O. R. Co.*, 93 Md. 475, 49 Atl. 327 (1901).

DECLARATION OF CORPORATE DIVIDEND?

dends is discretionary even in the case of a preferred stockholder, yet it is obvious that a preferred stockholder is entitled to more benign consideration in the eyes of a court of equity than a common stockholder, when he seeks to maintain an action to have a dividend declared. This is particularly the case where the preferred dividends are non-cumulative in character.[19]

Again, the stockholder in a "close" corporation is entitled to more favorable consideration than the stockholder in a corporation whose stock has a market value and is readily salable. If the stock of a stockholder can be readily sold in the open market, its market price would tend to increase *pari passu* as its book value increases and as the undistributed profits accumulate. The stockholder's share of the undistributed profits would be, in a sense, rendered to him year after year in the shape of a steady increment of the market value of his shares of stock, and the stockholder would be able, if necessary or if deemed desirable, from time to time to realize such part of his share of the annual accumulation of surplus profits as he might desire to take in the form of cash, by

[19] *Cratty* v. *Peoria Law Library Ass'n*, 219 Ill. 516, 76 N. E. 707 (1906).

MAY THE COURTS COMPEL

selling a few of his shares of stock in the open market. But, in the case of a "close" corporation, whose stock does not ordinarily possess any market value, it is generally difficult, if not impossible, to make sales of stock except upon disadvantageous terms. Therefore, the distinction between private close corporations, on the one hand, and large industrial or business corporations, the shares of which are readily salable at all times on the market, on the other hand, ought not to be overlooked by a court of equity in determining whether or not a dividend is being unreasonably, and therefore improperly, withheld from the stockholders.[20] It seems clear in the case of a "close" corporation that "where the directors roll their profits into their business from year to year until the great snowball has been magnified twenty diameters," it becomes the duty of a court of equity to interfere and compel the directors, under such circumstances, to declare a dividend for the benefit of the stockholders.[21]

The Louisiana cases upon this subject are illuminating and interesting, and deserve careful atten-

[20] *Raynolds* v. *Diamond Mills Paper Co.*, 69 N. J. Eq. 299, 60 Atl. 941 (1905).
[21] *Ibid.*

184

tion because of the unique character of the jurisprudence of the state. One of the earliest decisions
in point in the entire United States upon this topic
is the case of *State* v. *Bank of Louisiana*,[22] decided
in 1834. The state of Louisiana was interested in
the Bank of Louisiana, and complained in an action
commenced by the Attorney-General of the state,
in the name and for the use of the state, "that the
board (of directors of the bank) retains too large
a sum as a surplus to meet accidents and contin-
gencies." It appeared that the sum of $446,000
was kept on hand as a surplus, and the witnesses
differed as to the wisdom and reasonableness of re-
taining so large a sum on hand. The district judge
held that the board of directors ought to divide a
part of this large surplus among the stockholders,
and fixed the sum of $100,000 to be divided, and
ordered a dividend in said amount to be declared.
On appeal this ruling was reversed, and the appellate
court held that a very strong case must be made to
appear in order to induce a court to interfere with
the discretion of the corporation's board of directors,
and, as we have already seen, the court even inti-
mated that it is not clear that it has any power to
intervene at all, if the directors are honest.

[22] 6 La. 745.

MAY THE COURTS COMPEL

Martin, J., writing for the court, said:[23] "The charter has given the management of the affairs of the bank to the board of directors, and has expressly made it the judge of that portion of the profits, which it is advisable from time to time, to divide among the stockholders; a very strong case should indeed be made to justify a court in any interference with the management of these affairs, and to substitute its own judgment to that of the board on the *quantum* of the profits which it is proper to divide. If the board honestly err in these matters, we are not ready to say the courts possess the power to rectify its mistakes."

The court suggested[24] that "the remedy may be left to be applied by the stockholders, who at each annual election, have it in their power to change their agents."

In the well-known case of *Crichton* v. *Webb Press Co.*[25] it appears that a suit was brought by two minority stockholders to compel the defendant corporation to declare a dividend, which the board of directors had unreasonably and improperly refused to declare. The court ordered a dividend of

[23] 6 La. 745, at p. 763.
[24] *Ibid.*
[25] 113 La. 167, 36 So. 926, 67 L. R. A. 76, 104 Am. St. Rep. 500.

DECLARATION OF CORPORATE DIVIDEND?

$150,000 to be declared at once and paid to the stockholders in the proportions in which they were entitled to same. This case is cited frequently by the text writers.[26]

In the case of *Marks* v. *American Brewing Co.*,[27] a suit was brought by a minority stockholder to force the distribution of a corporate surplus among the stockholders. The evidence showed that dividends had been declared in past years largely because the surplus retained by the directors for the business of the corporation enabled it to operate on such a scale as to realize large profits. The court refused to order the declaration of a dividend.

Breaux, C. J., said: "We are not of the opinion, as relates to the distribution of dividends, that there should be any interference by the court unless it is manifestly evident that interference is necessary in the interest of the corporation and its shareholders. This court has always expressed unwillingness to interfere except where there was necessity as made evident by the testimony."

Referring to the early *Bank of Louisiana* case, the court said: "Even honest error will not be

[26] Clark on Corporations (3d ed.) 427, note 76.
[27] 126 La. 666, 52 So. 983.

187

rectified if the probabilities are that the board will be equal to correcting its mistakes."

It will be noted that this statement in the later case amounts to a plain intimation that even an honest error on the part of the board of directors in refusing to declare a dividend will be rectified if it is made to appear that the board of directors would not be apt voluntarily to correct its mistake. To that extent the dictum in the early case must be regarded as modified, if not overruled.

It is apparent from the opinion in the later case, read as an entirety, that the Louisiana court to-day would not hesitate to order the declaration of a dividend in a clear case, even in the absence of fraud or dishonesty on the part of the board. The court says: "It must be shown, in order to justify interference, that there is capricious, arbitrary or discriminating management. Only in proper case will the court interfere." It will be noted that the court does not limit its right to interfere to cases of fraud or dishonesty, but, on the contrary, states that it will interfere wherever the board is acting in an unreasonable manner, *e. g.*, where its refusal to declare a dividend is "capricious, arbitrary or discriminating."

The decision in the *Marks* case is a good practical

188

one, because the court points out with force, on the one hand, that a corporate surplus would amount to very little "if it were within the reach of the whim and caprice of every stockholder," and yet, at the same time, the court indicates that it will afford relief, even in the absence of fraud, wherever the circumstances are such as to justify equitable interference.

One other Louisiana decision deserves a word of comment. In the case of *Marcuse* v. *Gullett, etc., Co.,* [28] it was held that there was no need to appoint a special receiver in order to obtain relief, but that the individual stockholder has a full and adequate remedy through an action in his own name. This indicates the procedure to be adopted, namely, a stockholder's suit, as above suggested.

The writer trusts he has made it clear that the discretion of the board of directors with reference to the declaration of a dividend is ordinarily uncontrollable by the courts. It should not be lightly interfered with or readily disturbed. However, it is obvious that a court of equity can afford relief against dishonest or fraudulent conduct on the part of the directors, in this respect. It is also submitted that a court of equity likewise can and should afford

[28] 52 La. Ann. 1383, 27 So. 846 (1900).

relief against arbitrary or unreasonable conduct on the part of the directors, even though honest and free from fraud, since such conduct is equitably unjustifiable, and, therefore, warrants intervention. The wide discretionary powers of the board of directors must be employed not only in an honest manner, but also in a reasonable manner, and must never be employed in order to bring about the practical financial starvation of the stockholders, whose only sure hope of benefit from a corporate enterprise must come from the distribution of corporate profits in the form of dividends.

Index

191

INDEX

INDEX

193

INDEX

INDEX

FICTION.   See CORPORATE ENTITY; CORPORA-
TIONS.
corporate entity is not a, 8, 42.
corporate personality is a, 8, 42.
disregard of corporate, 18, 27, 28, 29, 30, 31, 32, 34, 35,
36, 37, 47, 48, 49, 50, 51, 52, 53, 54, 55, 56, 59, 60, 61,
62, 63, 64, 134.

FRAUD,
purchase by a corporation of its own stock as a, 125, 135,
136, 137.
declaration of dividends out of capital a, 137, 138, 139,
140.
corporation organized to perpetrate a, 28, 29, 30, 31, 47,
48, 49, 50, 51, 52, 53.

GRAND LARCENY,
criminal liability of corporation for, 4.

HEPBURN ACT,
explained and construed, 32, 33, 63, 64.

HOLMES, JUSTICE,
opinion in Brightman v. Bates, 147.

ILLEGAL CONTRACTS,
distinguished from ultra vires contracts, 135.

JOINT–STOCK ASSOCIATION,
definition, 101.
at common law, 101, 102, 106.
formation, 106.
purposes, 106, 107.
dissolution, 106, 107.
continuity of existence, 107.
common name, 107.
distinguished from a corporation, 101, 104, 108, 110, 111,
112, 115, 116, 117.

195

INDEX

INDEX

OFFICERS AND AGENTS,
    distinct from corporation, 11.
    powers of, 12, 174, 178, 185, 186, 190.

ONE MAN COMPANY. See CORPORATIONS; COR-
    PORATE ENTITY.
    corporation with sole stockholder, 14, 17, 18, 19, 20, 79,
        80, 81, 82, 83, 92.

PARTNERSHIP,
    formation of, 12, 106.
    purposes, 11, 12, 13.
    continuity of existence, 107.
    dissolution, 11, 12, 106.
    not an entity, 11, 14, 15.
    each partner agent for the, 12, 108.
    unlimited liability of, 13.
    common name, 107.
    distinguished from a corporation, 101, 102, 107.
    distinguished from a joint-stock association, 101, 102,
        104, 107, 112.

PERPETUAL SUCCESSION,
    faculty of, 11, 12, 107

PERSON,
    corporation as a, 4, 5, 7, 8, 9, 10, 15, 23, 27, 40, 42.

PIERCING THE VEIL OF CORPORATE ENTITY,
    what it means, 29, 30.

POOLING AGREEMENT. See VOTING TRUST.

POUND, DEAN,
    opinion in Home Fire Ins. v. Barber, 76.

POWERS OF A CORPORATION,
    to acquire and hold stock in another corporation, 86, 87,
        88, 89, 97, 120, 128, 129, 130, 131, 134, 135, 136, 137,
        140, 141.

INDEX

INDEX

www.ingramcontent.com/pod-product-compliance
Lightning Source LLC
Chambersburg PA
CBHW021556210326
41599CB00010B/466